B L O O M ' S

HOW TO WRITE ABOUT

Harper Lee

AMY WATKIN

Introduction by Harold Bloom

BLOOM'S
LITERARY CRITICISM
An imprint of Infobase Publishing

Bloom's How to Write about Harper Lee

Bloom's Literary Criticism
An imprint of Infobase Learning
132 West 31st Street
New York NY 10001

Library of Congress Cataloging-in-Publication Data
Watkin, Amy
   Bloom's how to write about Harper Lee / by Amy Watkin ; introduction by Harold Bloom.
      p. cm. — (Bloom's how to write about literature)
   Includes bibliographical references and index.
   ISBN 978-1-60413-746-0 (hardcover : alk. paper)
   1. Lee, Harper—Criticism and interpretation. 2. Criticism—Authorship. 3. Report writing. I. Bloom, Harold. II. Title.
   PS3562.E353Z94 2011
   813'.54—dc23

                                                                              2011020925

Bloom's Literary Criticism books are available at special discounts when purchased in bulk quantities for businesses, associations, institutions, or sales promotions. Please call our Special Sales Department in New York at (212) 967-8800 or (800) 322-8755.

You can find Bloom's Literary Criticism on the World Wide Web at
http://www.infobaselearning.com

Text design and composition by Annie O'Donnell
Cover design by Ben Peterson
Cover printed by Yurchak Printing, Landisville PA
Book printed and bound by Yurchak Printing, Landisville PA
Date printed: October 2011
Printed in the United States of America

10 9 8 7 6 5 4 3 2 1

All links and Web addresses were checked and verified to be correct at the time of publication. Because of the dynamic nature of the Web, some addresses and links may have changed since publication and may no longer be valid.

CONTENTS

SERIES INTRODUCTION

Bloom's How to Write about Literature series is designed to inspire students to write fine essays on great writers and their works. Each volume in the series begins with an introduction by Harold Bloom, meditating on the challenges and rewards of writing about the volume's subject author. The first chapter then provides detailed instructions on how to write a good essay, including how to find a thesis; how to develop an outline; how to write a good introduction, body text, and conclusions; how to cite sources; and more. The second chapter provides a brief overview of the issues involved in writing about the subject author and then a number of suggestions for paper topics, with accompanying strategies for addressing each topic. Succeeding chapters cover the author's major works.

The paper topics suggested in this book are open ended, and the brief strategies provided are designed to give students a push forward on the writing process rather than a road map to success. The aim of the book is to pose questions, not answer them. Many different kinds of papers could result from each topic. As always, the success of each paper will depend completely on the writer's skill and imagination.

HOW TO WRITE ABOUT HARPER LEE: INTRODUCTION

by Harold Bloom

I find that rereading *To Kill a Mockingbird* (wonderful title!) is, for me, a somewhat ambivalent experience. Scout Finch charms me, as she has so many millions of people, and yet she seems to me better than her book, which has dated into a period piece, while she herself remains remarkably vital and refreshing. Since Scout *is* her book, I find my own reaction an enigma, and hope to enlighten at least myself in this introduction. No one could expect Scout to rival Huck Finn (from whom she serenely derives), and yet her sensibility, intelligence, and decency strongly recall aspects of Huck. This, I think, is all to the good: a younger, female Huckleberry Finn fills a void in American fiction. The aesthetic problem is not Scout Finch, but her father, Atticus, and the entire range of major and minor characters in the story. Atticus and all the others are ideograms rather than people, while Harper Lee's portrait of the artist as a young girl has the individuality, of consciousness and of speech, that allows the representation of a person to be much more than a name on a page.

Harper Lee cannot sustain comparison with Eudora Welty and Flannery O'Connor, or even with Carson McCullers. It would be wrong to make such a contrast, except that to see the limits of *To Kill a Mockingbird* is also to perceive better the novel's relative success in portraying Scout Finch. It is very difficult to represent any healthy consciousness in

vii

literature, whether we are being shown an eight-year-old girl or a fully mature woman. Shakespeare, most prodigious of all writers ever, has an astonishing triumph in the Rosalind of *As You Like It*, a heroine who is not only a superb wit, like Falstaff and Hamlet, but who manifests an absolutely normative consciousness, free of all neuroses and darknesses. As an audience, we cannot achieve any perspectives upon Rosalind in which she has not preceded us. She sees all around, as it were, and has a largeness that inspired Jane Austen to emulation. A wholesome sensibility attracts us in life, yet rarely confronts us in literature. One cannot expect Scout Finch to grow up into Rosalind; Scout is perceptive and quick, but her mind is essentially conventional. And yet her spirit is free, in a kind of proto-feminist variation upon Huck Finn's.

The story that Scout tells is circumscribed by time and by region, and also by an America before the Fall, in our final Age of Innocence, the 1950s. Harper Lee and her book emerged from a country yet to experience the Vietnam War and the subsequent advent of the counterculture. The United States is a nation desperately losing faith in all authority, whether governmental or familial. *To Kill a Mockingbird*, in its societal aspects, is already a period piece, and its faith in essential human nature can seem very naive. The book's continued popularity, still extraordinary, partly suggests that we find in it a study of the nostalgias. Yet nostalgia itself dates; the reader becomes alienated from it, when nothing restores a sense of its relevance. There remains the portrait of Scout Finch. Her voice, for now, retains immediacy, and speaks for and to many among us. Whether she will survive the aspects of her story that time has staled, I cannot prophesy.

HOW TO WRITE
A GOOD ESSAY

By Laurie A. Sterling and Amy Watkin

While there are many ways to write about literature, most assignments for high school and college English classes call for analytical papers. In these assignments, you are presenting your interpretation of a text to your reader. Your objective is to interpret the text's meaning in order to enhance your reader's understanding and enjoyment of the work. Without exception, strong papers about the meaning of a literary work are built on a careful, close reading of the text or texts. Careful, analytical reading should always be the first step in your writing process. This volume provides models of such close, analytical reading, and these should help you develop your own skills as a reader and as a writer.

As the examples throughout this book demonstrate, attentive reading entails thinking about and evaluating the formal (textual) aspects of the author's works: theme, character, form, and language. In addition, when writing about a work, many readers choose to move beyond the text itself to consider the work's cultural context. In these instances, writers might explore the historical circumstances of the time period in which the work was written. Alternatively, they might examine the philosophies and ideas that a work addresses. Even in cases where writers explore a work's cultural context, though, papers must still address the more formal aspects of the work itself. A good interpretative essay that evaluates Charles Dickens's use of the philosophy of utilitarianism in his novel *Hard Times,* for example, cannot adequately address the author's treatment of the philosophy without firmly grounding this discussion in the book itself. In other words, any analytical paper about a text, even one that seeks to evaluate the work's cultural context, must also have a firm handle on the work's themes, characters, and language. You must look for and evaluate these aspects of a work, then, as you read a text and as you prepare to write about it.

WRITING ABOUT THEMES

Literary themes are more than just topics or subjects treated in a work; they are attitudes or points about these topics that often structure other elements in a work. Writing about theme therefore requires that you not just identify a topic that a literary work addresses but also discuss what that work says about that topic. For example, if you were writing about the culture of the American South in William Faulkner's famous story "A Rose for Emily," you would need to discuss what Faulkner says, argues, or implies about that culture and its passing.

When you prepare to write about thematic concerns in a work of literature, you will probably discover that, like most works of literature, your text touches on other themes in addition to its central theme. These secondary themes also provide rich ground for paper topics. A thematic paper on "A Rose for Emily" might consider gender or race in the story. While neither of these could be said to be the central theme of the story, they are clearly related to the passing of the "old South" and could provide plenty of good material for papers.

As you prepare to write about themes in literature, you might find a number of strategies helpful. After you identify a theme or themes in the story, you should begin by evaluating how other elements of the story—such as character, point of view, imagery, and symbolism—help develop the theme. You might ask yourself what your own responses are to the author's treatment of the subject matter. Do not neglect the obvious, either: What expectations does the title set up? How does the title help develop thematic concerns? Clearly, the title "A Rose for Emily" says something about the narrator's attitude toward the title character, Emily Grierson, and all she represents.

WRITING ABOUT CHARACTER

Generally, characters are essential components of fiction and drama. (This is not always the case, though; Ray Bradbury's "August 2026: There

Will Come Soft Rains" is technically a story without characters, at least any human characters.) Often, you can discuss character in poetry, as in T. S. Eliot's "The Love Song of J. Alfred Prufrock" or Robert Browning's "My Last Duchess." Many writers find that analyzing character is one of the most interesting and engaging ways to work with a piece of literature and to shape a paper. After all, characters generally are human, and we all know something about being human and living in the world. While it is always important to remember that these figures are not real people but creations of the writer's imagination, it can be fruitful to begin evaluating them as you might evaluate a real person. Often you can start with your own response to a character. Did you like or dislike the character? Did you sympathize with the character? Why or why not?

Keep in mind, though, that emotional responses like these are just starting places. To truly explore and evaluate literary characters, you need to return to the formal aspects of the text and evaluate how the author has drawn these characters. The twentieth-century writer E. M. Forster coined the terms *flat* characters and *round* characters. Flat characters are static, one-dimensional characters who frequently represent a particular concept or idea. In contrast, round characters are fully drawn and much more realistic characters who frequently change and develop over the course of a work. Are the characters you are studying flat or round? What elements of the characters lead you to this conclusion? Why might the author have drawn characters like this? How does their development affect the meaning of the work? Similarly, you should explore the techniques the author uses to develop characters. Do we hear a character's own words, or do we hear only other characters' assessments of him or her? Or, does the author use an omniscient or limited omniscient narrator to allow us access to the workings of the characters' minds? If so, how does that help develop the characterization? Often you can even evaluate the narrator as a character. How trustworthy are the opinions and assessments of the narrator? You should also think about characters' names. Do they mean anything? If you encounter a hero named Sophia or Sophie, you should probably think about her wisdom (or lack thereof), since *sophia* means "wisdom" in Greek. Similarly, since the name *Sylvia* is derived from the word *sylvan,* meaning "of the wood," you might want to evaluate that character's relationship with nature. Once again, you might look to the title of the work. Does Herman Melville's "Bartleby, the Scrivener" signal anything about Bartleby himself? Is Bartleby adequately defined by his job as scrivener? Is this part of Melville's point? Pursuing questions like these can help you develop thorough papers about characters from psychological, sociological, or more formalistic perspectives.

WRITING ABOUT FORM AND GENRE

Genre, a word derived from French, means "type" or "class." Literary genres are distinctive classes or categories of literary composition. On the most general level, literary works can be divided into the genres of drama, poetry, fiction, and essays, yet within those genres there are classifications that are also referred to as genres. Tragedy and comedy, for example, are genres of drama. Epic, lyric, and pastoral are genres of poetry. *Form,* on the other hand, generally refers to the shape or structure of a work. There are many clearly defined forms of poetry that follow specific patterns of meter, rhyme, and stanza. Sonnets, for example, are poems that follow a fixed form of 14 lines. Sonnets generally follow one of two basic sonnet forms, each with its own distinct rhyme scheme. Haiku is another example of poetic form, traditionally consisting of three unrhymed lines of five, seven, and five syllables.

While you might think that writing about form or genre might leave little room for argument, many of these forms and genres are very fluid. Remember that literature is evolving and ever changing, and so are its forms. As you study poetry, you may find that poets, especially more modern poets, play with traditional poetic forms, bringing about new effects. Similarly, dramatic tragedy was once quite narrowly defined, but over the centuries playwrights have broadened and challenged traditional definitions, changing the shape of tragedy. When Arthur Miller wrote *Death of a Salesman,* many critics challenged the idea that tragic drama could encompass a common man like Willy Loman.

Evaluating how a work of literature fits into or challenges the boundaries of its form or genre can provide you with fruitful avenues of investigation. You might find it helpful to ask why the work does or does not fit into traditional categories. Why might Miller have thought it fitting to write a tragedy of the common man? Similarly, you might compare the content or theme of a work with its form. How well do they work together? Many of Emily Dickinson's poems, for instance, follow the meter of traditional hymns. While some of her poems seem to express traditional religious doctrines, many seem to challenge or strain against traditional conceptions of God and theology. What is the effect, then, of her use of traditional hymn meter?

WRITING ABOUT LANGUAGE, SYMBOLS, AND IMAGERY

No matter what the genre, writers use words as their most basic tool. Language is the most fundamental building block of literature. It is essential that you pay careful attention to the author's language and word choice as you read, reread, and analyze a text. Imagery is language that appeals to the senses. Most commonly, imagery appeals to our sense of vision, creating a mental picture, but authors also use language that appeals to our other senses. Images can be literal or figurative. Literal images use sensory language to describe an actual thing. In the broadest terms, figurative language uses one thing to speak about something else. For example, if I call my boss a snake, I am not saying that he is literally a reptile. Instead, I am using figurative language to communicate my opinions about him. Since we think of snakes as sneaky, slimy, and sinister, I am using the concrete image of a snake to communicate these abstract opinions and impressions.

The two most common figures of speech are similes and metaphors. Both are comparisons between two apparently dissimilar things. Similes are explicit comparisons using the words *like* or *as;* metaphors are implicit comparisons. To return to the previous example, if I say, "My boss, Bob, was waiting for me when I showed up to work five minutes late today—the snake!" I have constructed a metaphor. Writing about his experiences fighting in World War I, Wilfred Owen begins his poem "Dulce et decorum est" with a string of similes: "Bent double, like old beggars under sacks, / Knock-kneed, coughing like hags, we cursed through sludge." Owen's goal was to undercut clichéd notions that war and dying in battle were glorious. Certainly, comparing soldiers to coughing hags and to beggars underscores his point.

"Fog," a short poem by Carl Sandburg provides a clear example of a metaphor. Sandburg's poem reads:

The fog comes
on little cat feet.

It sits looking
over harbor and city
on silent haunches
and then moves on.

Notice how effectively Sandburg conveys surprising impressions of the fog by comparing two seemingly disparate things—the fog and a cat.

Symbols, by contrast, are things that stand for, or represent, other things. Often they represent something intangible, such as concepts or ideas. In everyday life we use and understand symbols easily. Babies at christenings and brides at weddings wear white to represent purity. Think, too, of a dollar bill. The paper itself has no value in and of itself. Instead, that paper bill is a symbol of something else, the precious metal in a nation's coffers. Symbols in literature work similarly. Authors use symbols to evoke more than a simple, straightforward, literal meaning. Characters, objects, and places can all function as symbols. Famous literary examples of symbols include Moby Dick, the white whale of Herman Melville's novel, and the scarlet *A* of Nathaniel Hawthorne's *The Scarlet Letter.* As both of these symbols suggest, a literary symbol cannot be adequately defined or explained by any one meaning. Hester Prynne's Puritan community clearly intends her scarlet *A* as a symbol of her adultery, but as the novel progresses, even her own community reads the letter as representing not just *adultery,* but *able, angel,* and a host of other meanings.

Writing about imagery and symbols requires close attention to the author's language. To prepare a paper on symbolism or imagery in a work, identify and trace the images and symbols and then try to draw some conclusions about how they function. Ask yourself how any symbols or images help contribute to the themes or meanings of the work. What connotations do they carry? How do they affect your reception of the work? Do they shed light on characters or settings? A strong paper on imagery or symbolism will thoroughly consider the use of figures in the text and will try to reach some conclusions about how or why the author uses them.

WRITING ABOUT HISTORY AND CONTEXT

As noted above, it is possible to write an analytical paper that also considers the work's context. After all, the text was not created in a vacuum.

The author lived and wrote in a specific time period and in a specific cultural context and, like all of us, was shaped by that environment. Learning more about the historical and cultural circumstances that surround the author and the work can help illuminate a text and provide you with productive material for a paper. Remember, though, that when you write analytical papers, you should use the context to illuminate the text. Do not lose sight of your goal—to interpret the meaning of the literary work. Use historical or philosophical research as a tool to develop your textual evaluation.

Thoughtful readers often consider how history and culture affected the author's choice and treatment of his or her subject matter. Investigations into the history and context of a work could examine the work's relation to specific historical events, such as the Salem witch trials in seventeenth-century Malden, Massachusetts, or the restoration of Charles to the British throne in 1660. Bear in mind that historical context is not limited to politics and world events. While knowing about the Vietnam War is certainly helpful in interpreting much of Tim O'Brien's fiction, and some knowledge of the French Revolution clearly illuminates the dynamics of Charles Dickens's *A Tale of Two Cities*, historical context also entails the fabric of daily life. Examining a text in light of gender roles, race relations, class boundaries, or working conditions can give rise to thoughtful and compelling papers. Exploring the conditions of the working class in nineteenth-century England, for example, can provide a particularly effective avenue for writing about Dickens's *Hard Times*.

You can begin thinking about these issues by asking broad questions at first. What do you know about the time period and about the author? What does the editorial apparatus in your text tell you? These might be starting places. Similarly, when specific historical events or dynamics are particularly important to understanding a work but might be somewhat obscure to modern readers, textbooks usually provide notes to explain historical background. These are a good place to start. With this information, ask yourself how these historical facts and circumstances might have affected the author, the presentation of theme, and the presentation of character. How does knowing more about the work's specific historical context illuminate the work? To take a well-known example, understanding the complex attitudes toward slavery during the time Mark Twain wrote *Adventures of Huckleberry Finn* should help you begin to examine issues of race in the text. Additionally, you might compare these attitudes to those of the time in which the novel was set. How might this comparison affect your interpretation of a work written after the abolition of slavery but set before the Civil War?

WRITING ABOUT PHILOSOPHY AND IDEAS

Philosophical concerns are closely related to both historical context and thematic issues. Like historical investigation, philosophical research can provide a useful tool as you analyze a text. For example, an investigation into the working class in Dickens's England might lead you to a topic on the philosophical doctrine of utilitarianism in *Hard Times*. Many other works explore philosophies and ideas quite explicitly. Mary Shelley's famous novel *Frankenstein*, for example, explores John Locke's tabula rasa theory of human knowledge as she portrays the intellectual and emotional development of Victor Frankenstein's creature. As this example indicates, philosophical issues are somewhat more abstract than investigations of theme or historical context. Some other examples of philosophical issues include human free will, the formation of human identity, the nature of sin, or questions of ethics.

Writing about philosophy and ideas might require some outside research, but usually the notes or other material in your text will provide you with basic information and often footnotes and bibliographies suggest places you can go to read further about the subject. If you have identified a philosophical theme that runs through a text, you might ask yourself how the author develops this theme. Look at character development and the interactions of characters, for example. Similarly, you might examine whether the narrative voice in a work of fiction addresses the philosophical concerns of the text.

WRITING COMPARISON AND CONTRAST ESSAYS

Finally, you might find that comparing and contrasting the works or techniques of an author provides a useful tool for literary analysis. A comparison and contrast essay might compare two characters or themes in a single work, or it might compare the author's treatment of a theme in two works. It might also contrast methods of character development or analyze an author's differing treatment of a philosophical concern in two works. Writing comparison and contrast essays, though, requires some special consideration. While they generally provide you with plenty of material to use, they also come with a built-in trap: the laundry list. These papers often become mere lists of connections between the works. As this chapter will discuss, a strong thesis must make an assertion that you want to prove or validate. A strong comparison/contrast thesis, then, needs to comment on the significance of the similarities and differences you observe. It is not enough merely to assert that the works contain similarities and differences. You might, for example, assert why the similarities and differences are important and explain how they illuminate the works' treatment of theme. Remember, too, that a thesis should not be a statement of the obvious. A comparison/contrast paper that focuses only on very obvious similarities or differences does little to illuminate the connections between the works. Often, an effective method of shaping a strong thesis and argument is to begin your paper by noting the similarities between the works but then to develop a thesis that asserts how these apparently similar elements are different. If, for example, you observe that Emily Dickinson wrote a number of poems about spiders, you might analyze how she uses spider imagery differently in two poems. Similarly, many scholars have noted that Hawthorne created many "mad scientist" characters, men who are so devoted to their science or their art that they lose perspective on all else. A good thesis comparing two of these characters—Aylmer of "The Birth-mark" and Dr. Rappaccini of "Rappaccini's Daughter," for example—might initially identify both characters as examples of Hawthorne's mad scientist type but then argue that their motivations for scientific experimentation differ. If you strive to analyze the similarities or differences, discuss significances, and move beyond the obvious, your paper should move beyond the laundry list trap.

PREPARING TO WRITE

Armed with a clear sense of your task—illuminating the text—and with an understanding of theme, character, language, history, and philosophy, you are ready to approach the writing process. Remember that good writing is grounded in good reading and that close reading takes time, attention, and more than one reading of your text. Read for comprehension first. As you go back and review the work, mark the text to chart the details of the work as well as your reactions. Highlight important passages, repeated words, and image patterns. "Converse" with the text through marginal notes. Mark turns in the plot, ask questions, and make observations about characters, themes, and language. If you are reading from a book that does not belong to you, keep a record of your reactions in a journal or notebook. If you have read a work of literature carefully, paying attention to both the text and the context of the work, you have a leg up on the writing process. Admittedly, at this point, your ideas are probably very broad and undefined, but you have taken an important first step toward writing a strong paper.

Your next step is to focus, to take a broad, perhaps fuzzy, topic and define it more clearly. Even a topic provided by your instructor will need to be focused appropriately. Remember that good writers make the topic their own. There are a number of strategies—often called "invention"—that you can use to develop your own focus. In one such strategy, called *freewriting*, you spend 10 minutes or so just writing about your topic without referring back to the text or your notes. Write whatever comes to mind; the important thing is that you just keep writing. Often this process allows you to develop fresh ideas or approaches to your subject matter. You could also try *brainstorming*: Write down your topic and then list all the related points or ideas you can think of. Include questions, comments, words, important passages or events, and anything else that comes to mind. Let one idea lead to another. In the related technique of *clustering*, or *mapping*, write your topic on a sheet of paper and write related ideas around it. Then list related subpoints under each of these main ideas. Many people then draw arrows to show connections between points. This technique helps you narrow your topic and can also help you organize your ideas. Similarly, asking journalistic questions—Who? What? Where? When? Why? and How?—can develop ideas for topic development.

Thesis Statements

Once you have developed a focused topic, you can begin to think about your thesis statement, the main point or purpose of your paper. It is imperative that you craft a strong thesis; otherwise, your paper will likely be little more than random, disorganized observations about the text. Think of your thesis statement as a kind of road map for your paper. It tells your reader where you are going and how you are going to get there.

To craft a good thesis, you must keep a number of things in mind. First, as the title of this subsection indicates, your paper's thesis should be a statement, an assertion about the text that you want to prove or validate. Beginning writers often formulate a question that they attempt to use as a thesis. For example, a writer exploring racism in Lee's *To Kill a Mockingbird* might ask, What role does race play in the novel? While a question like this is a good strategy to use in the invention process to help narrow your topic and find your thesis, it cannot serve as the thesis statement because it does not tell your reader what you want to assert about race. You might shape this question into a thesis by instead proposing an answer to that question: In Harper Lee's novel *To Kill a Mockingbird*, racial injustice and social class cause the death of Tom Robinson. Notice that this thesis provides an initial plan or structure for the rest of the paper. After discussing racism, you could examine the ways in which racist attitudes are presented as inevitable in this novel and then theorize about what Lee is saying about racism more generally.

Second, remember that a good thesis makes an assertion that you need to support. In other words, a good thesis does not state the obvious. If you tried to formulate a thesis about racism by simply saying, Race is important in *To Kill a Mockingbird*, you have done nothing but rephrase the obvious. Since Lee's novel is partly centered on racial issues, there would be no point in spending three to five pages supporting that assertion. You might try to develop a thesis from that point by asking yourself some further questions: What does it mean when any given character expresses a racist attitude? Does the novel seem to indicate that racism is inevitable? Does it present racism as an advantage, or is racism always negative in this novel? Such a line of questioning might lead you to a more viable thesis, like the one in the preceding paragraph.

As the comparison with the road map also suggests, your thesis should appear near the beginning of the paper. In relatively short papers (three to six pages) the thesis almost always appears in the first paragraph. Some writers fall into the trap of saving their thesis for the end, trying to provide a surprise or a big moment of revelation, as if to say, "TA-DA! I've just proved that in *An Ideal Husband,* Oscar Wilde uses the snake brooch to symbolize Mrs. Cheveley's true character." Placing a thesis at the end of an essay can seriously mar the essay's effectiveness. If you fail to define your essay's point and purpose clearly at the beginning, your reader will find it difficult to assess the clarity of your argument and understand the points you are making. When your argument comes as a surprise at the end, you force your reader to reread your essay in order to assess its logic and effectiveness.

Finally, you should avoid using the first person ("I") as you present your thesis. Though it is not strictly wrong to write in the first person, it is difficult to do so gracefully. While writing in the first person, beginning writers often fall into the trap of writing self-reflexive prose (writing *about* their paper *in* their paper). Often this leads to the most dreaded of opening lines: "In this paper I am going to discuss . . ." Not only does this self-reflexive voice make for very awkward prose, but it frequently allows writers to boldly announce a topic while completely avoiding a thesis statement. An example might be a paper that begins as follows: Harper Lee's To Kill a Mockingbird takes place in small town southern America, where supposedly nothing much happens. In this paper I am going to discuss how the women in the novel react to Atticus's decisions and the children's adventures with Boo Radley. The author of this paper has done little more than announce a general topic for the paper. While the last sentence might be a thesis, the writer fails to present an opinion about the significance of the reaction. To improve this "thesis," the writer would need to back up a couple of steps. First, the announced topic of the paper is too broad; it largely summarizes the events in the story without saying anything about the ideas in the story. The writer should highlight what she considers the meaning of the story: What is the story about? The writer might conclude that the children's antics create feelings of fear in the women. From here, the author could select the means by which Lee communicates these ideas and then begin to craft a specific thesis. A writer who chooses to explore the symbols of fear that are associated with women might, for example, craft a thesis that reads, In To Kill a Mockingbird, Harper Lee emphasizes the fear surrounding racism in the South through her characterizations of women.

Outlines

While developing a strong, thoughtful thesis early in your writing process should help focus your paper, outlining provides an essential tool for logically shaping that paper. A good outline helps you see—and develop—the relationships among the points in your argument and assures you that your paper flows logically and coherently. Outlining not only helps place your points in a logical order but also helps you subordinate supporting points, weed out any irrelevant points, and decide if there are any necessary points that are missing from your argument. Most of us are familiar with formal outlines that use numerical and letter designations for each point. However, there are different types of outlines; you may find that an informal outline is a more useful tool for you. What is important, though, is that you spend the time to develop some sort of outline—formal or informal.

Remember that an outline is a tool to help you shape and write a strong paper. If you do not spend sufficient time planning your supporting points and shaping the arrangement of those points, you will most likely construct a vague, unfocused outline that provides little, if any, help with the writing of the paper. Consider the following example.

Thesis: In Harper Lee's novel *To Kill a Mockingbird*, racial injustice and social class cause the death of Tom Robinson

    I. Introduction and thesis

   II. Scout's childhood

  III. Tom Robinson

  IV. Boo Radley

   V. Social class
       A. Education
       B. Bob Ewell
       C. Race
       D. Jem

  VI. Conclusion

> A. Tom was convicted because his race made
>   him part of the lowest social class, and
>   social class was important to people

This outline has a number of flaws. First, the major topics labeled with the Roman numerals are not arranged in a logical order. If the paper's focus is on Tom Robinson, the writer should establish the particulars of his character and situation before showing how Scout's childhood plays a role. Similarly, the thesis makes no reference to Boo Radley. The writer includes his name as a major section of this outline but fails to provide details about his place in the argument. Third, the writer includes Jem's character as one of the lettered items in section V. Letters A, B, and C all refer to specific instances where the concept of social class will be discussed; Jem does not belong in this list. A fourth problem is the inclusion of a section A in section VI. An outline should not include an A without a B, a 1 without a 2, and so forth. The final problem with this outline is the overall lack of detail. None of the sections provide much information about the content of the argument, and it seems likely that the writer has not given sufficient thought to the content of the paper.

A better start to this outline might be the following:

Thesis: In Harper Lee's novel *To Kill a Mockingbird*, racial injustice and social class cause the death of Tom Robinson

    I. Introduction and thesis

   II. Tom Robinson
         A. Mayella Ewell
         B. Atticus's legal arguments

  III. Racism
         A. Atticus's closing arguments
         B. Education

   IV. Social class
         A. The Ewells
         B. Calpurnia

```
V. Conclusion
   A. Tom was convicted because his race made
      him part of the lowest social class, and
      social class was important to people
```

This new outline would prove much more helpful when it came time to write the paper.

An outline like this could be shaped into an even more useful tool if the writer fleshed out the argument by providing specific examples from the text to support each point. Once you have listed your main point and your supporting ideas, develop this raw material by listing related supporting ideas and material under each of those main headings. From there, arrange the material in subsections and order the material logically.

For example, you might begin with one of the theses cited above: In Harper Lee's novel *To Kill a Mockingbird*, racial injustice and social class cause the death of Tom Robinson. As previously noted, this thesis already gives you the beginning of an organization: Start by providing the necessary background about racism and Lee's views and then explain how Lee presents racism. You might begin your outline, then, with three topic headings: (1) Tom Robinson, (2) racism, and (3) social class. Under each of those headings you could list ideas that support the particular point. Be sure to include references to parts of the text that help build your case.

An informal outline might look like this:

```
Thesis: In Harper Lee's novel To Kill a Mockingbird,
racial injustice and social class cause the death of
Tom Robinson

  1. Tom Robinson
     • Mayella Ewell's accusations
     • Atticus definitively proves Mayella wrong

  2. Tom loses because of his race
     • Atticus's closing arguments
     • "Ain't ever seen any jury decide in favor
       of a colored man" (Lee 208)
```

- Calpurnia—How is she treated by the Finch family?

3. Differences in society
   - The Ewells
   - "Ewells had been the disgrace of Maycomb for three generations" (Lee 30)
   - Ties between social class and race

4. Conclusion
   - Tom was convicted because his race made him part of the lowest social class, and social class was important to people

You would set about writing a formal outline with a similar process, though in the final stages you would label the headings differently. A formal outline for a paper that argues the thesis about *To Kill a Mockingbird* cited above might look like this:

Thesis: In Harper Lee's novel *To Kill a Mockingbird*, racial injustice and social class cause the death of Tom Robinson

   I. Introduction and thesis

  II. Tom Robinson
       A. Mayella Ewell's accusations
       B. Atticus's arguments in court

 III. Racism
       A. Atticus's closing arguments
       B. "Ain't ever seen any jury decide in favor of a colored man" (Lee 208)

  IV. Social class
       A. The Ewells

```
        B. "Ewells had been the disgrace of Maycomb
           for three generations" (Lee 30)
        C. Ties between social class and race

  V. Conclusion
        A. Tom was convicted because his race made
           him part of the lowest social class, and
           social class was important to people
```

As in the previous example outline, the thesis provided the seeds of a structure, and the writer was careful to arrange the supporting points in a logical manner, showing the relationships among the ideas in the paper.

Body Paragraphs

Once your outline is complete, you can begin drafting your paper. Paragraphs, units of related sentences, are the building blocks of a good paper, and as you draft you should keep in mind both the function and the qualities of good paragraphs. Paragraphs help you chart and control the shape and content of your essay, and they help the reader see your organization and your logic. You should begin a new paragraph whenever you move from one major point to another. In longer, more complex essays you might use a group of related paragraphs to support major points. Remember that in addition to being adequately developed, a good paragraph is both unified and coherent.

Unified Paragraphs

Each paragraph must be centered on one idea or point, and a unified paragraph carefully focuses on and develops this central idea without including extraneous ideas or tangents. For beginning writers, the best way to ensure that you are constructing unified paragraphs is to include a topic sentence in each paragraph. This topic sentence should convey the main point of the paragraph, and every sentence in the paragraph should relate to that topic sentence. Any sentence that strays from the central topic does not belong in the paragraph and needs to be revised or deleted. Consider the following paragraph about racism in *To Kill a*

Mockingbird. Notice how the paragraph veers away from the main point that racism led to Tom Robinson's death:

> Racism affected Tom Robinson's case and led him to his death. He was convicted of rape even though Atticus proved that his case couldn't even happen. First of all, Mayella Ewell had a blackened right eye, and someone who is left handed strikes on the right side. In Maycomb, members of upper social classes look down on members of lower social classes. The Ewells are lower class, and people do not think well of them. For example, Atticus explains to Scout why she should stay in school by using them as an example: "Ewells had been the disgrace of Maycomb for three generations" (30), he says. Aunt Alexandra also does not think highly of lower classes; when Scout wants to play with Walter Cunningham, she tells Scout that "Finch women aren't interested in that sort. . . . Because—he—is—trash" (224–25).

Although the paragraph begins solidly, and the first sentence provides the central idea of the paragraph, the author soon goes on a tangent. If the purpose of the paragraph is to demonstrate that racism plays an integral role in the novel, the sentences about the Ewells and social class are tangential here. They may find a place later in the paper, but they should be deleted from this paragraph.

Coherent Paragraphs

In addition to shaping unified paragraphs, you must also craft coherent paragraphs, paragraphs that develop their points logically with sentences that flow smoothly into one another. Coherence depends on the order of your sentences, but it is not strictly the order of the sentences that is important to paragraph coherence. You also need to craft your prose to help the reader see the relationship among the sentences.

Consider the following paragraph about racism in *To Kill a Mockingbird.* Notice how the writer uses the same ideas as the paragraph above yet fails to help the reader see the relationships among the points.

Racism affected Tom Robinson's case and led him to his death. He was convicted of rape even though Atticus proved that his case couldn't even happen. First of all, Mayella Ewell had a blackened right eye, and someone who is left handed strikes on the right side. Mayella hesitates when she is asked if she remembers Tom hitting her in the face (185). Tom was still found guilty. "In our court when it's a white man's word against a black man's, the white man always wins," Atticus states (220). After Atticus's closing argument, Jem thinks his father will win, but Reverend Sykes mentions that he "ain't ever seen any jury decide in favor of a colored man over a white man"(208).

This paragraph demonstrates that unity alone does not guarantee paragraph effectiveness. The argument is hard to follow because the author fails both to show connections between the sentences and to indicate how they work to support the overall point.

A number of techniques are available to aid paragraph coherence. Careful use of transitional words and phrases is essential. You can use transitional flags to introduce an example or an illustration (*for example, for instance*), to amplify a point or add another phase of the same idea (*additionally, furthermore, next, similarly, finally, then*), to indicate a conclusion or result (*therefore, as a result, thus, in other words*), to signal a contrast or a qualification (*on the other hand, nevertheless, despite this, on the contrary, still, however, conversely*), to signal a comparison (*likewise, in comparison, similarly*), and to indicate a movement in time (*afterward, earlier, eventually, finally, later, subsequently, until*).

In addition to transitional flags, careful use of pronouns aids coherence and flow. If you were writing about *The Wizard of Oz*, you would not want to keep repeating the phrase *the witch* or the name *Dorothy*. Careful substitution of the pronoun *she* in these instances can aid coherence. A word of warning, though: When you substitute pronouns for proper names, always be sure that your pronoun reference is clear. In a paragraph that discusses both Dorothy and the witch, substituting *she* could lead to confusion. Make sure that it is clear to whom the pronoun refers. Generally, the pronoun refers to the last proper noun you have used.

While repeating the same name over and over again can lead to awkward, boring prose, it is possible to use repetition to help your paragraph's coherence. Careful repetition of important words or phrases can lend coherence to your paragraph by reminding readers of your key points. Admittedly, it takes some practice to use this technique effectively. You may find that reading your prose aloud can help you develop an ear for effective use of repetition.

To see how helpful transitional aids are, compare the paragraph below to the preceding paragraph about racism in *To Kill a Mockingbird.* Notice how the author works with the same ideas and quotations but shapes them into a much more coherent paragraph whose point is clearer and easier to follow.

> Racism affected Tom Robinson's case and led him to his death. He was convicted of rape even though Atticus proved that his case couldn't even happen. First of all, Mayella Ewell had a blackened right eye, and someone who is left handed strikes on the right side. Bob Ewell was a drunk, and he was left handed. Secondly, the sheriff and Bob Ewell didn't get a doctor to check on Mayella. Also, Tom Robinson can't use his left hand. Finally, Mayella hesitates when she is asked if she remembers Tom hitting her in the face (185), which is a sign that she is lying. Even with all these facts, Tom was still found guilty. "In our court when it's a white man's word against a black man's, the white man always wins," Atticus states (220). Other people in the community feel this way, too. After Atticus's closing argument, Jem thinks his father will win, but Reverend Sykes mentions that he "ain't ever seen any jury decide in favor of a colored man over a white man"(208). Even though it is clear he did not do it, Tom Robinson was convicted because of his skin color, which is tied to his social class.

Introductions

Introductions present particular challenges for writers. Generally, your introduction should do two things: capture your reader's attention and explain the main point of your essay. In other words, while your introduction should contain your thesis, it needs to do a bit more work than that. You are likely to find that starting that first paragraph is one of the most difficult parts of the paper. It is hard to face that blank page or screen, and as a result, many beginning writers, in desperation to start somewhere, start with overly broad, general statements. While it is often a good strategy to start with more general subject matter and narrow your focus, do not begin with broad sweeping statements such as Everyone likes to be creative and feel understood. Such sentences are nothing but empty filler. They begin to fill the blank page, but they do nothing to advance your argument. Instead, you should try to gain your readers' interest. Some writers like to begin with a pertinent quotation or with a relevant question. Or, you might begin with an introduction of the topic you will discuss. If you are writing about Lee's presentation of racism in *To Kill a Mockingbird,* for instance, you might begin by talking about definitions of racism. Another common trap to avoid is depending on your title to introduce the author and the text you are writing about. Always include the work's author and title in your opening paragraph.

Compare the effectiveness of the following introductions.

1. Throughout history, people of various races have been oppressed. Think how you feel when you really want something: It makes you feel bad when you don't get it, right? In this story, Lee shows characters' different points of view about race. More importantly, she shows how racism functions.

2. Do you think that status is an important thing? Will it help you make friends and get people on your side? What about race? Can it give you advantages and disadvantages? Does it affect how people look at you? Now consider whether race and class help to decide who is guilty and who is not. In Harper Lee's novel *To Kill a Mockingbird*, racial injustice and social class cause the death of Tom Robinson. Racism affected Tom Robinson's case and led him to his

death. He was convicted of rape even though Atticus
proved that his case couldn't even happen.

The first introduction begins with a vague, overly broad sentence; cites unclear, undeveloped examples; and then moves abruptly to the very weak thesis. Notice, too, how a reader deprived of the paper's title does not know the title of the story that the paper will analyze. The second introduction works with the same material and thesis but provides more detail and is consequently much more interesting. The paragraph ends with the thesis. This effective introduction also includes the title of the text and full name of the author.

Conclusions

Conclusions present another series of challenges for writers. No doubt you have heard the adage about writing papers: "Tell us what you are going to say, say it, and then tell us what you've said." While this formula does not necessarily result in bad papers, it does not often result in good ones, either. It will almost certainly result in boring papers (especially boring conclusions). If you have done a good job establishing your points in the body of the paper, the reader already knows and understands your argument. There is no need to merely reiterate. Do not just summarize your main points in your conclusion. Such a boring and mechanical conclusion does nothing to advance your argument or interest your reader. Consider the following conclusion to the paper about racism in *To Kill a Mockingbird*.

In conclusion, Lee uses the concept of racism in her
novel. Tom Robinson is an example. Lee shows some
interpretations of racism through her characterizations.
We should all remember that.

Besides starting with a mechanical transitional device, this conclusion does little more than summarize the main points of the outline (and it does not even touch on all of them). It is incomplete and uninteresting.

Instead, your conclusion should add something to your paper. A good tactic is to build upon the points you have been arguing. Asking "why?" often helps you draw further conclusions. For example, in the paper on

To Kill a Mockingbird, you might speculate or explain how the concept of racism speaks to how Lee is presenting characters in the novel in order to convey her beliefs about racism. Another method for successfully concluding a paper is to speculate on other directions in which to take your topic by tying it into larger issues. You might do this by envisioning your paper as just one section of a larger paper. Having established your points in this paper, how would you build upon this argument? Where would you go next? In the following conclusion to the paper on *To Kill a Mockingbird,* the author reiterates some of the main points of the paper but does so in order to amplify the discussion of the novel's central message:

> Tom was convicted because his race made him part of the lowest social class and social class was important to people. Because of this belief, many people in the town felt that the verdict was right. Scout states that "in the secret court of men's hearts Atticus had no case. Tom was a dead man the minute Mayella Ewell opened her mouth and screamed" (Lee 241). This was only because Tom was black and Mayella was white. If it was now Tom would have been not guilty, especially with no evidence. It was surprising that Atticus was the only white man who had the courage to go against these beliefs and defend Tom Robinson. He was the only one brave enough to point out this problem when he said, "you'll see white men cheat black men every day . . . whenever a white man does that to a black man, no matter who he is . . . that white man is trash" (Lee 220).

Citations and Formatting

Using Primary Sources

As the examples included in this chapter indicate, strong papers on literary texts incorporate quotations from the text in order to support their points. It is not enough for you to assert your interpretation without providing support or evidence from the text. Without well-chosen quotations to support your argument you are, in effect, saying to the reader, "Take my word for it." It is important to use quotations thoughtfully and selectively. Remember that the paper presents *your* argument, so choose quotations that support *your* assertions. Do not let the author's voice overwhelm your own. With that caution in mind, there are some guidelines you should follow to ensure that you use quotations clearly and effectively.

Integrate Quotations:

Quotations should always be integrated into your own prose. Do not just drop them into your paper without introduction or comment. Otherwise, it is unlikely that your reader will see their function. You can integrate textual support easily and clearly with identifying tags, short phrases that identify the speaker. For example:

> Jack responds, "Oh, pleasure, pleasure!"

While this tag appears before the quotation, you can also use tags after or in the middle of the quoted text, as the following examples demonstrate:

> "What else should bring one anywhere?" asks Jack.

> "I have only been married once," Lane tells Algernon. "That was in consequence of a misunderstanding between myself and a young person."

You can also use a colon to formally introduce a quotation:

> It is clear that Algernon takes offense: "I believe it is customary in good society to take some slight refreshment at five o'clock."

When you quote brief sections of poems (three lines or fewer), use slash marks to indicate the line breaks in the poem:

> As the poem ends, Dickinson speaks of the power of the imagination: "The revery alone will do, / If bees are few."

Longer quotations (more than four lines of prose or three lines of poetry) should be set off from the rest of your paper in a block quotation. Double-space before you begin the passage, indent it 10 spaces from your left-hand margin, and double-space the passage itself. Because the indentation signals the inclusion of a quotation, do not use quotation marks around the cited passage. Use a colon to introduce the passage:

Maycomb becomes almost a character right at the beginning:

> People moved slowly then. They ambled across the square, shuffled in and out of the stores around it, took their time about everything. A day was twenty-four hours long but seemed longer. There was no hurry, for there was nowhere to go, nothing to buy and no money to buy it with, nothing to see outside the boundaries of Maycomb County.

Clearly, the pace of life in Maycomb will play a role in this novel.

The whole of Dickinson's poem speaks of the imagination:

> To make a prairie it takes a clover and one bee,
> One clover, and a bee,
> And revery.
> The revery alone will do,
> If bees are few.

Clearly, she argues for the creative power of the mind.

It is also important to interpret quotations after you introduce them and explain how they help advance your point. You cannot assume that your reader will interpret the quotations the same way that you do.

Quote Accurately

Always quote accurately. Anything within quotation marks must be the author's exact words. There are, however, some rules to follow if you need to modify the quotation to fit into your prose.

1. Use brackets to indicate any material that might have been added to the author's exact wording. For example, if you need to add any words to the quotation or alter it grammatically to allow it to fit into your prose, indicate your changes in brackets:

    ```
    Jack counters Algernon's suggestion by stating,
    "There is no good offering a reward now that
    the [cigarette case] is found."
    ```

2. Conversely, if you choose to omit any words from the quotation, use ellipses (three spaced periods) to indicate missing words or phrases:

    ```
    Jack tells Algernon, "I have been writing frantic
    letters . . . about it."
    ```

3. If you delete a sentence or more, use the ellipses after a period:

    ```
    Algernon defends himself to Jack: "It isn't. . . .
    It accounts for the extraordinary number of
    bachelors that one sees all over the place."
    ```

4. If you omit a line or more of poetry, or more than one paragraph of prose, use a single line of spaced periods to indicate the omission:

    ```
    To make a prairie it takes a clover and one bee,
    .  .  .  .  .  .  .  .  .  .  .  .  .  .  .  .  .  .
    And revery.
    The revery alone will do,
    If bees are few.
    ```

Punctuate Properly

Punctuation of quotations often causes more trouble than it should. Once again, you just need to keep these simple rules in mind.

1. Periods and commas should be placed inside quotation marks, even if they are not part of the original quotation:

   ```
   Jack admits the truth to Lady Bracknell: "I have
   lost both my parents."
   ```

   The only exception to this rule is when the quotation is followed by a parenthetical reference. In this case, the period or comma goes after the citation (more on these later in this chapter):

   ```
   Jack admits the truth to Lady Bracknell: "I have
   lost both my parents" (2,189).
   ```

2. Other marks of punctuation—colons, semicolons, question marks, and exclamation points—go outside the quotation marks unless they are part of the original quotation:

   ```
   Why does Lady Bracknell tell Jack that "to lose
   both seems like carelessness"?
   ```

Documenting Primary Sources

Unless you are instructed otherwise, you should provide sufficient information for your reader to locate material you quote. Generally, literature papers follow the rules set forth by the Modern Language Association (MLA). These can be found in the *MLA Handbook for Writers of Research Papers* (seventh edition). You should be able to find this book in the reference section of your library. Additionally, its rules for citing both primary and secondary sources are widely available from reputable online sources. One of these is the Online Writing Lab (OWL) at Purdue University. OWL's guide to MLA style is available at http://owl.english. purdue.edu/owl/resource/557/01/. The Modern Language Association also offers answers to frequently asked questions about MLA style on this helpful Web page: http://www.mla.org/style_faq. Generally, when you are citing from literary works in papers, you should keep a few guidelines in mind.

Parenthetical Citations:

MLA asks for parenthetical references in your text after quotations. When you are working with prose (short stories, novels, or essays) include page numbers in the parentheses:

> Algernon defends himself to Jack: "It isn't. . . . It accounts for the extraordinary number of bachelors that one sees all over the place" (2,180).

When you are quoting poetry, include line numbers:

> Dickinson's speaker tells of the arrival of a fly: "There interposed a Fly— / With Blue—uncertain stumbling Buzz— / Between the light—and Me—" (12-14).

Works Cited Page:

These parenthetical citations are linked to a separate works cited page at the end of the paper. The works cited page lists works alphabetically by the authors' last name. An entry for the preceding reference to Wilde's *The Importance of Being Earnest* would read:

> Wilde, Oscar. "The Importance of Being Earnest." *The Norton Anthology: English Literature.* Ed. M.H. Abrams, and Stephen Greenblatt. New York: W. W. Norton and Co., 2001. 2,177-2,223.

The *MLA Handbook* includes a full listing of sample entries, as do many of the online explanations of MLA style.

Documenting Secondary Sources

To ensure that your paper is built entirely upon your own ideas and analysis, instructors often ask that you write interpretative papers without any outside research. If, on the other hand, your paper requires research, you must document any secondary sources you use. You need to document direct quotations, summaries or paraphrases of others' ideas, and factual information that is not common knowledge. Follow the guidelines above for quoting primary sources when you use direct quotations from secondary sources. Keep in mind that MLA style also includes specific guidelines for citing electronic sources. OWL's Web site provides a good summary: http://owl.english.purdue.edu/owl/resource/557/09/.

Parenthetical Citations:

As with the documentation of primary sources, described above, MLA guidelines require in-text parenthetical references to your secondary sources. Unlike the research papers you might write for a history class, literary research papers following MLA style do not use footnotes as a means of documenting sources. Instead, after a quotation, you should cite the author's last name and the page number:

Jack admits the truth to Lady Bracknell: "I have lost both my parents" (Wilde 2,189).

If you include the name of the author in your prose, then you would include only the page number in your citation. For example:

Clearly Wilde intends for Algernon to take offense: "I believe it is customary in good society to take some slight refreshment at five o'clock" (2,179).

If you are including more than one work by the same author, the parenthetical citation should include a shortened yet identifiable version of the title in order to indicate which of the author's works you cite. For example:

Clearly Wilde intends for Algernon to take offense: "I believe it is customary in good society to take some slight refreshment at five o'clock" (*Importance* 2,179).

Similarly, and just as important, if you summarize or paraphrase the particular ideas of your source, you must provide documentation:

```
Jack agrees with Algernon but is not ready to admit it
(Wilde 2,180).
```

Works Cited Page:

Like the primary sources discussed above, the parenthetical references to secondary sources are keyed to a separate works cited page at the end of your paper. Here is an example of a works cited page that uses the examples cited above. Note that when two or more works by the same author are listed, you should use three hyphens followed by a period in the subsequent entries. You can find a complete list of sample entries in the *MLA Handbook* or from a reputable online summary of MLA style.

WORKS CITED

Holcomb, Briavel. "Women Travellers at Fins de Siecles." *Focus* 43 (Winter 1993): 11–15. Academic Search Premier. 23 April 2006

"The New Woman." *Clash of Cultures.* 2005. Ohio State University History Department. 23 April 2006.

Parker, Oliver, dir. *The Importance of Being Earnest.* Miramax: 2002.

Richardson, Angelique. "The Eugenization of Love." *University of Exeter* (1999): 228–259.

Wilde, Oscar. "The Importance of Being Earnest." *The Norton Anthology: English Literature.* Ed. M.H. Abrams, and Stephen Greenblatt. New York: W. W. Norton and Co., 2001. 2,177–2,223.

Plagiarism

Failure to document carefully and thoroughly can leave you open to charges of stealing the ideas of others, which is known as plagiarism, and this is a very serious matter. Remember that it is important to include quotation marks when you use language from your source, even if you use just one or two words. For example, if you wrote, Algernon believes it is customary in good society, you would be guilty of plagiarism, since you used Wilde's distinct language without acknowledging him as the source. Instead, you should write: Algernon says that "it is customary in good society to take some slight refreshment at five o'clock" (Wilde 2,179).

In this case, you have properly credited Wilde.

Similarly, neither summarizing the ideas of an author nor changing or omitting just a few words means that you can omit a citation. Vyvyan Holland's book *Son of Oscar Wilde* contains the following passage:

> Most small boys adore their fathers, and we adored ours; and as all good fathers are, he was a hero to us both. . . . There was nothing about him of the monster that some people who never knew him and never even saw him have tried to make him out to be. He was a real companion to us, and we always looked forward eagerly to his frequent visits to our nursery. Most parents in those days were far too solemn and pompous with their children, insisting on a vast amount of usually undeserved respect. My own father was quite different; he had so much of the child in his own nature that he delighted in playing our games. (52)

Below are two examples of plagiarized passages:

Vyvyan Holland loved his father and, like a lot of kids, really looked up to him. He did not know the vicious person that many people believed Wilde to be. All he knew was that his father was not serious and overly inflated like many parents.

Holland contends that his father was quite different, especially given the fact that he was very much a child in his own nature (Holland 52).

While the first passage does not use Holland's exact language, it does list some of the same examples as the book. Since this interpretation is Holland's distinct idea, this constitutes plagiarism. The second passage has shortened his passage, changed some wording, and included a citation, but some of the phrasing is Holland's. The first passage could be fixed with a parenthetical citation. Because some of the wording in the second remains the same, though, it would require the use of quotation marks, in addition to a parenthetical citation. The passage below represents an honestly and adequately documented use of the original passage:

> Vyvyan Holland remembers his childhood very fondly: "Most small boys adore their fathers, and we adored ours; and as all good fathers are, he was a hero to us both. . . . There was nothing about him of the monster that some people who never knew him and never even saw him have tried to make him out to be" (52).

This passage acknowledges that the interpretation is derived from Holland while appropriately using quotations to indicate his precise language.

While it is not necessary to document well-known facts, often referred to as "common knowledge," any ideas or language that you take from someone else must be properly documented. Common knowledge generally includes the birth and death dates of authors or other well-documented facts of their lives. An often-cited guideline is that if you can find the information in three sources, it is common knowledge. Despite this guideline, it is, admittedly, often difficult to know if the facts you uncover are common knowledge or not. When in doubt, document your source.

Sample Essay

Ronald Sundstrom, Jr.
Chelsie Thielen
Champlin Park High School
May 23, 2011

THE TRUTH ABOUT TOM ROBINSON

Do you think that status is an important thing? Will it help you make friends and get people on your side? What about race? Can it give you advantages and disadvantages? Does it affect how people view you? Now consider whether race and class help to decide who is guilty and who is not. In Harper Lee's novel *To Kill a Mockingbird*, racial injustice and social class cause the death of Tom Robinson.

Racism affected Tom Robinson's case and led him to his death. He was convicted of rape even though Atticus proved that his case couldn't even happen. First of all, Mayella Ewell had a black eye on her right, and someone who is lefthanded strikes on the right side. Bob Ewell was a drunk, and he was lefthanded. Secondly, the sheriff and Bob Ewell didn't get a doctor to check on Mayella. Also, Tom Robinson can't use his left hand. Finally, Mayella hesitates when she is asked if she remembers Tom hitting her in the face (Lee 185), which is a sign that she is lying. Even with all these facts, Tom was still found guilty. "In our court when it's a White man's word against a Black man's, the white man wins," Atticus states (Lee 220). Other people in the community feel this way too. After Atticus' closing argument, Jem thinks his father will win, but Reverend Sykes mentions that he "ain't ever seen any jury decide in favor of a colored man over a white man" (Lee 208). Even though it is clear he did not do it, Tom Robinson was convicted because of his skin color, which is tied to his social class.

In Maycomb, members of upper social classes look down on members of lower social classes. The Ewells are lower class, and people do not think well of them. For example, Scout related Atticus's sentiments on why she should stay in school by using them as an example: "Ewells had been the disgrace of Maycomb for three generations," he says (Lee 30). Aunt Alexandra also does not think highly of lower classes; when Scout wants to play with Walter Cunningham, she tells Scout that "Finch women aren't interested in that sort. . . . Because—he—is—trash" (Lee 224-25). But the Ewells are still higher than Tom Robinson because he is black. Back then, all black people were considered lower-class citizens, whether they had money or not.

Tom was convicted because his race made him part of the lowest social class, and social class was important to people. Because of this belief, many people in the town felt that the verdict was right. Scout states that "in the secret court of men's hearts Atticus had no case. Tom was a dead man the minute Mayella Ewell opened her mouth and screamed" (Lee 241). This was only because Tom was black and Mayella was white. If it was now, Tom would have been not guilty, especially with no evidence. It was surprising that Atticus was the only white man who had the courage to go against these beliefs and defend Tom Robinson. He was the only one brave enough to point out this problem when he said, "you'll see white men cheat black men every day . . . whenever a white man does that to a black man, no matter who he is . . . that white man is trash" (Lee 220).

WORKS CITED

Lee, Harper. *To Kill a Mockingbird*. 1960. New York: Harper Perennial Modern Classics, 2006. Print.

HOW TO WRITE ABOUT HARPER LEE

HER LEGACY

It took Harper Lee two and a half years to write *To Kill a Mockingbird*, and the novel was published July 11, 1960, and would be awarded the Pulitzer Prize the following year. Selling more than 500,000 copies in the first six months, the book did not take long to become "the most popular novel in American literature in the twentieth century, and . . . readers rank [it] in surveys as the most influential in their lives after the Bible" (Shields *Mockingbird* 202). Since its debut, "the book has sold nearly 40 million copies worldwide—becoming one of the most successful novels in publishing history—and has now been translated into more than 40 languages. A staple of high school and college reading lists, it ranked fourth in a Fall 1991 survey on 'Books that Made a Difference in Reader's Lives,' conducted by the Book-of-the-Month Club and the Library of Congress" (Taylor 26). Many American students recall reading the book in high school, because "by 1988 the book 'was taught in 74 percent of the nation's public schools'—a statistic issued by the National Council of Teachers of English" (Mallon 82).

Yet Harper Lee never set out to become a famous author. She has largely shunned the fame that comes with this literary popularity. Her aspirations, while lofty, did not include fame and fortune:

> I want to do the best I can with the talent God gave me. I hope to good-
> ness that every novel I do gets better and better, not worse and worse. I
> would like, however, to do one thing, and I've never spoken much about

it because it's such a personal thing. I would like to leave some record of the kind of life that existed in a very small world. I hope to do this in several novels—to chronicle something that seems to be very quickly going down the drain. This is small-town middle-class southern life as opposed to the Gothic, as opposed to *Tobacco Road,* as opposed to plantation life. As you know, the South is still made up of thousands of tiny towns. There is a very definite social pattern in these towns that fascinates me. I think it is a rich social pattern. I would simply like to put down all I know about this because I believe that there is something universal in this little world, something decent to be said for it, and something to lament in its passing. In other words all I want to be is the Jane Austen of south Alabama. (Newquist 412)

She knew she had something different to say about a way of life and area of the country that had already been chronicled, to some extent. Harper Lee certainly did "leave some record of the kind of life that existed in a very small world," and this record seems to be one in which readers from various backgrounds find commonality.

In the previously cited quotation, Harper Lee seems to know more about what *To Kill a Mockingbird,* or her writing in general, is not than she knows about what it is. She does not, however, question the ambition to write more than one novel. She mentions that she would like to write "several novels," and that she would like to be "the Jane Austen of south Alabama." Jane Austen wrote six novels. Although what Lee seems to be suggesting in using this comparison is Austen's noteworthy style of writing about the day-to-day minutia of small groups of people in particular social and financial circumstances. She did not concern herself with world events or large populations.

These words of Lee's also clue us in to her attitude toward the South, her home. Certainly elements of *To Kill a Mockingbird* are critical of the region, its traditions and habits, but underneath that is a love story of sorts. The "rich social pattern" of this part of the United States is a significant part of the novel, and while terrible things happen in Maycomb, readers are still left feeling nostalgic for a time and a place that Lee conveys so carefully as to make it seem familiar, even to those who have never been to the South.

On December 25, 1962, the film version of *To Kill a Mockingbird*, starring Gregory Peck, opened in theaters. Harper Lee was a part of the film's production and has since expressed sincere approval for the film-makers' interpretations of her novel. Audiences also approved: "In the most recent polls by the American Film Institute, *To Kill a Mockingbird* was ranked #25 on the list of Greatest American Films of all time and #2 on the list of Most Inspiring Movies (just behind *It's a Wonderful Life*) . . . in a related ranking by the AFI, Gregory Peck's portrayal earned the honor as 'Greatest Hero in 100 Years of Film History'" (Taylor 26).

Today there is a band called Harper Lee, because the members had originally planned to release only one album. The National Endowment for the Arts, through its Big Read program, produced a half-hour radio show discussion of *To Kill a Mockingbird* that is available on the Internet and includes commentary from Robert Duvall, one of the actors in the movie, as well as Charles J. Shields, author of the first full-length biography of Harper Lee, among others. The novel has also been adapted into a stage production, and the play is regularly performed. *Boo* is a new play put on by Mind the Gap, a theater company from the United Kingdom that works with learning disabled artists: "[T]he production asks what happens if, like Boo, you don't fit in. Set in a modern estate, the show is a tale of two children who are fascinated and terrified of the 'bogeyman' they can't see" (Barr).

Why, then, hasn't Harper Lee written more than one novel? This is the most pressing question and the prominent issue concerning Lee's legacy. Surely such a talented writer is not going to torture her legions of fans by writing only one book? This was not Lee's intention. Before *To Kill a Mockingbird* was published, she had already written 111 pages of a second novel, titled *The Long Goodbye*. When asked in a 1963 interview how she felt about her second novel, Lee responded, "I'm scared" ("1963 Chicago").

HER INFLUENCES

Harper Lee makes the adage "write what you know" come to life in a way that few others have accomplished. When you peel back the layers behind the Finch family in Maycomb, Alabama, you begin to reveal details about the Lee family in Monroeville, Alabama.

Writing was important to Lee's family, evidenced in part by the fact that, until 1947, they owned the *Monroe Journal*. The law, however, was more important to the family. Lee's father, A.C., and her sister, Alice, both entered the field of law. Lee began law school but did not finish, determining finally that she had no passion for the career. She paid attention to the law throughout her life, however, spending time in the Monroe County courthouse: "From the gallery, Truman and Nelle could watch Mr. Lee below performing the functions of a title lawyer. Truman later complained that sometimes Nelle only seemed interested in hanging around the courthouse and playing golf" (Shields 50).

Why does this book linger in its readers' minds long after they have finished it? Why do so many people come back to it, reading it many times? Why is it so often taught in high schools? In some ways, it is the fact that this story had already been told so many times that makes *To Kill a Mockingbird* stand out:

> the novel was a 'mixture of ingredients that ought to guarantee a bad novel. The story is told from the point of view of an eight-year-old child; it is set in the kind of Southern small town that has been described in fiction a thousand times; the characters are exactly the types that a correspondence-school course in fiction would prescribe for a Southern small-town novel. . . . The denouement is pure Gothic fiction.' But . . . 'Miss Lee remembers much of what she has seen, heard, and felt; she has discriminating feelings and judgments about what she has seen and heard; she knows what to tell and what to leave out; and she must have worked hard at the craft of putting words to paper. *To Kill a Mockingbird* is a superior book because it was written by a superior person who became a professional writer without inflicting her apprenticeship on the public in a trial book.' (qtd. in Shields *Mockingbird* 201–02)

From certain angles, Harper Lee and *To Kill a Mockingbird* are inseparable. It seems clear that her greatest inspiration for the novel was the world around her—the American South.

Charles Shields writes that "[t]he level of dinner table conversation at the Lees' was probably more elevated than what was normal in most small-town households in Alabama" (*Mockingbird* 75). We see this elevated conversation at the Finch table too. Lee was certainly influenced by Truman Capote, who lived next door to her in the summers and after whom she modeled the character of Dill. Capote would go on to write *In Cold Blood,* among many other successful works. Certainly Lee was also influenced by writers she read and loved. In a 1963 interview, she says she reads "mostly 19th century, rather than 20th century, writers. Charles Lamb, Jane Austin [sic], Thackeray . . . all that crowd" ("1963 Chicago"). But mainly, Lee is influenced by her family, her town, and the relatively small world that surrounds her.

HER WORK

Lee's work as a whole clearly shows the influences of her professional and personal life. A familiarity with her background, however, is not necessary for doing intriguing analysis of Lee's work. This volume will guide you through general approaches to her fiction. The remainder of this section will discuss some of the notable elements of Lee's work: the patterns in her use of themes; her construction of character; the history and context of her writing; the philosophy underlying her book; and her use of symbolism, imagery, and language.

Themes

The temptation with a book like *To Kill a Mockingbird* is to boil it down to one overly simplistic and often moralistic theme, when the reality is that the work conveys any number of simple and complex themes about people, life, and the nature of the world.

The most obvious themes in the novel surround race, though as Edgar Schuster writes, "If *Mockingbird* is primarily a race relations novel, why is it that the author gives such a full treatment to episodes that seem totally unrelated to this theme?" (507). Perhaps because the novel is also about tolerance, justice, courage, insanity, redemption, education, control, superstition, honor, compassion, and innocence.

Some of these themes may be the reason *To Kill a Mockingbird* has frequently appeared on banned book lists. The themes are complicated and difficult, often displaying a darker side that few of us care to see or reflect on as part of our own consciousness. To this end, we cannot ignore the race issues that threaten to engulf the novel at times. An important question to ask about race-related themes such as tolerance, victimization, prejudice, and justice is this: What is Harper Lee trying to convey through these themes? Are these themes exclusively concerned with race, or do they reflect other issues as well, such as class, gender, or religion? Is Lee always critical of racial injustice, or does the novel at times uphold a "separate but equal" view of the world? It seems that Lee was not looking for easy answers through *To Kill a Mockingbird*. Perhaps she was instead hoping to raise these types of questions.

Characters

Whether it is through the novel or the film, the characters in *To Kill a Mockingbird* are vividly drawn and thus memorable personages in the history of American literature. Their names invoke particular feelings and expectations. Atticus Finch is honorable, respectable, and heroic. Scout is curious, innocent, and wise. Tom Robinson is victimized yet noble. Yet even these characters may be more complicated than they first appear.

We might ask ourselves what Scout comes to represent. Childhood? Innocence? The process of growing up? Is she an amalgamation of children everywhere, or is she a representation of just one particular child, or neither?

We know that Harper Lee based some of her characters on real people. Atticus Finch is clearly modeled after Lee's father, A.C. Lee. Harper Lee's mother's maiden name was Finch, bringing the characters even closer to Lee's reality. Tom Robinson's trial is understood to have been taken from the headlines, reflecting the Scottsboro Boys as well as the Emmett Till trial. Scout, we assume, embodies Lee's own childhood, and this relationship explains in part why Lee chooses to write the novel from essentially two points of view: Scout as a child and Scout as an adult. Yet the novel is never classified as autobiography or memoir, leaving us to wonder what good it does to know that many characters are based on real people and whether any novel can ever be entirely fictional.

To Kill a Mockingbird "is written out of Harper Lee's love for the South and Monroeville, but it is also the story of a father's love for his children, and the love they gave in return" (Hendrix 1B). Readers enjoy debating whether or not Atticus is the central character in the novel. We see and experience much of the action through Scout's eyes, and yet the world we are made privy to is very often Atticus's world. Is there an argument to be made that Tom Robinson or Boo Radley are the novel's main protagonists?

Form and Genre

Apart from its treatment of race, the most controversial thing about *To Kill a Mockingbird* seems to be its point of view. Lee chose to center the novel on Scout's and Jem's coming-of-age stories, inserting adult wisdom in ways that some have called genius and others have regarded as jarring and unnecessary. Both sides, however, agree that the coming-of-age element holds the novel together and is part of what draws readers again and again:

> "*To Kill a Mockingbird* could have bombed at the time on the issue of race," said Lucinda MacKethan, a Southern literature professor at North Carolina State University and co-editor of *The Companion to Southern Literature*. "The White South was still benighted in its outlook on race when the book came out, and Lee's honest, sympathetic treatment of this one area could have made the novel less popular. But the one thing she did to make her angle very different, and not just judgmental, right off the bat, was to make this a story of coming-of-age—the confrontation of innocence with experience, which is the universal story." (Taylor 28)

In this way, Lee writes more than just a novel. She writes about the evolution of a life, a process to which all American readers can relate. Judging by the number of translations, it would seem that even non-American readers can relate to the coming-of-age themes the tale foregrounds.

Language, Symbols, and Imagery

One of the first things many readers decide at the outset of a novel is whether or not they will trust the narrator. In the case of *To Kill a Mockingbird*, who wouldn't trust little Scout? Yet in this novel, readers essentially encounter two narrators: young Scout and adult Jean Louise. Are either of them reliable? Are both of them reliable? How can we tell? How we answer these questions can dictate how we internalize the rest of the book.

Symbolism in *To Kill a Mockingbird* is evident from the title. This is not a book about murdering birds, and we may realize that even before

Lee demonstrates this in the novel's dialogue. (It may be relevant to note, in some essays, that the original title was *Go Set a Watchman*, which was changed to *Atticus* and finally to *To Kill a Mockingbird*.) But what does the mockingbird represent? Boo Radley? Tom Robinson? Both? All African Americans? Likewise, we might ask what Jem and Scout's snowman represents. Lee has made sure that larger forces and ideas are at work through these relatively straightforward actions and discussions. It becomes our job as readers to decipher them and apply our own context and interpretations.

History and Context

To Kill a Mockingbird "seemed to have tapped into the important concerns of the era—the burgeoning interest in civil rights for blacks, the appeal of life set in simpler, pre-cold war times, and the need on the part of Americans to see themselves as justice-loving in the face of communism" (Shields *Mockingbird* 183). The context in which Lee writes and sets this novel is pivotal to our understanding and also one of the reasons the book has been banned at times through the years.

Lee was clearly conversant with and attuned to the American (specifically southern) events occurring at the time that she wrote *To Kill a Mockingbird*. What, then, did she intend to convey through the novel? Was she attempting to influence social change? If so, what sorts of change does she advocate? Reading the novel as a commentary on social events and conditions of the American South in the 1950s might make us wonder if the immediate and enduring popularity of the novel speaks to the fact that citizens were ready to hear Lee's message for change. To that end, does Lee's novel inspire further reform? Is there evidence that *To Kill a Mockingbird* drove readers to affect changes in their own lives and communities?

Another fascinating aspect of history and context lies in the consideration of the novel's context and influence today. In what sort of context is *To Kill a Mockingbird* taught in the twenty-first century? Maybe students are taught that the book encapsulates a period of American history, or perhaps they are taught that the book is timeless in its values and themes. The book is even used as a catalyst to inspire change, even today.

Philosophy and Ideas

In a 1963 interview, Lee stated, "The book is not an indictment so much as a plea for something, a reminder to people at home" ("1963 Chicago"). Of what was Lee hoping to remind "people at home"? The philosophies and ideas that surface throughout *To Kill a Mockingbird* provide some clues as to the hopes Lee may have had for her novel.

There are a number of all-encompassing, nearly universal ideas and philosophies on which Lee concentrates in this novel. When Scout and Aunt Alexandra weave through their relationship threads of resentment, expectation, and grudging respect, we are left to consider ideas of gender and one's place in the world. We can look at the different "parenting" styles of Calpurnia and Atticus to examine respect, moral values, the importance of teaching, and gender roles. Of course studying Tom Robinson's trial affords us an opportunity to pursue written law versus moral law and the time and place for each.

Comparison and Contrast

Any comparison or contrast study of *To Kill a Mockingbird* might do well to start with the film adaptation of the book. Understanding that change must occur in the transition from one medium to another, we can certainly come to some conclusions about how successfully the movie encapsulates the book and which form resonates with us more.

If we remain exclusively within the realm of the novel, we can still find a wide range of opportunities for comparisons and contrasts. Consider whether Calpurnia and Atticus are more alike than they are different. Perhaps as she grows up Scout undergoes significant changes in her attitude and belief systems, or perhaps she changes very little. A biographical study can lead us to compare and contrast Lee's real influences with the characters in the book. How similar, for example, are A.C. Lee and Atticus Finch? What might those similarities and differences reveal about Lee's relationship with her father, her attitude toward lawyers, or her understanding of the world? Or if we delve into the theme of appearance versus reality, we can compare and contrast the real Boo Radley with the Boo invented by the children and the townspeople.

Conclusion

Harper Lee is, of course, still alive, begging the question of whether she has written or ever will write anything more. If she did publish another novel, would it expand her influence or tarnish her legacy? Perhaps the fact that *To Kill a Mockingbird* stands alone has become a part of its appeal and capacity to endure. Or maybe the film's influence is what has really set the novel apart. We may never find answers to these questions, though somehow it seems likely that this fact, and the persistence of life questions that surround the book, keep a sly grin on Lee face.

Bibliography and Online Resources

"1963 Chicago Press Call." *Rogue*, vol. 8, no. 12: (December 1963). Posted on Jane Kansas Web site, 25 May 2004.

Lee, Harper. *To Kill a Mockingbird*. 1960. New York: Harper Perennial Modern Classics, 2006. Print.

Newquist, Roy. "Harper Lee." *Counterpoint*. New York: Simon and Schuster, 1964. 404–12.

Schuster, Edgar H. "Discovering Theme and Structure in the Novel." *The English Journal*, vol. 52, no. 7 (October 1963): 506–11.

Shields, Charles J. *Mockingbird: A Portrait of Harper Lee*. New York: Holt Paperbacks, 2007.

Taylor, Art. "Do the Right Thing: Harper Lee and *To Kill a Mockingbird*." *Mystery Scene*, no. 101 (Fall 2007): 22–28.

HOW TO WRITE ABOUT
TO KILL A
MOCKINGBIRD

HISTORY OF *TO KILL A MOCKINGBIRD*

Few books throughout history have been as beloved as *To Kill a Mockingbird*. Few have been as controversial. It speaks to Lee's achievement that the book is able to wrap us in a world at once familiar, comforting, and starkly, startlingly wrong. What do we know about Lee's process in conceiving and writing it and then revising the manuscript for publication? What has the American (and international) love/hate relationship with *To Kill a Mockingbird* really entailed?

> Within a few weeks after the publication party in New York in July, *To Kill a Mockingbird* hit both the *New York Times* and the *Chicago Tribune* lists of top ten bestsellers. Reviewers for major publications—who would generally cast a skeptical eye on tales about virtue standing up to evil and peppered with homespun verities about life—found themselves enchanted by *To Kill a Mockingbird*. (Shields *Mockingbird* 182)

Even Lee seems reluctant to garner even more notoriety from a novel that has become more of a cultural movement than a mere book. Where does *To Kill a Mockingbird* fit on the spectrum of literature, when first published as well as more recently? Why is it so often a part of the curriculum in American high schools?

It is appropriate and even necessary, when studying a phenomenon like *To Kill a Mockingbird*, to look outside the book itself and investigate the circumstances of its production and reception through the years.

Strategies

This section of the chapter addresses various possible topics for writing about the history of *To Kill a Mockingbird* as well as general methods for approaching these topics. These lists are in no way exhaustive and are meant to provide a jumping-off point rather than an answer key. Use these suggestions to find your own ideas and form your own analyses. All topics discussed in this chapter could turn into strong, effective papers.

Sample Topics:

1. **Revisions:** What changes did the *To Kill a Mockingbird* manuscript undergo before publication?

   It is fascinating to think about the changes that Lee and her editors made to the novel before its publication. We know that early in the review process, editors felt that "on the one hand, her 'characters stood on their own two feet, they were three-dimensional.' On the other, the manuscript had structural problems: it was 'more a series of anecdotes than a fully conceived novel'" (Shields *Mockingbird* 115). Then we read that for the second revision "[t]here were dangling threads of plot, there was a lack of unity" (qtd in Shields *Mockingbird* 116) and that "All [Lee] hoped for was a 'quick and merciful death at the hands of reviewers'" (Shields *Mockingbird* 175). How do we regard the novel differently after learning the details about its revision process? Do we see Lee's literary choices as more deliberate and painstaking, rather than the easily found results of a writing genius?

2. **Censorship:** Why has *To Kill a Mockingbird* so often been censored in some way?

In 1966, citizens of Hanover, Virginia, argued that the book contained inappropriate subject matter (an alleged rape), and the school board removed it from the county's school libraries, inciting public debate. Since then a number of schools and organizations have protested the book for the following reasons: "the portrayal of conflict between children and their elders, or children questioning the wisdom of their elders; profanity or questionable language; ungrammatical speech by characters; use of black dialect; references to the supernatural or witchcraft; depictions of violence; references to sex; negative statements about persons in authority, the United States, or American traditions; the lack of portrayal of a family unit as the basis of American life; and unfavorable presentations of blacks" (Johnson 15). Is *To Kill a Mockingbird* currently on any banned book lists? Why or why not? What does the book's history of censorship reveal about American society, our concepts of and presumptions about literature, and/or how and why Americans read? What is it that the reading public, educators, and librarians expect from literature? Do those expectations change when the literature is popular?

3. **Critical reception:** How have reviewers and the reading public in general responded to *To Kill a Mockingbird* over the years?

The critical reception of *To Kill a Mockingbird* has been evolving through the years, though in general it has been relatively positive—so positive, in fact, that we have to wonder if some of the negative reception has been written simply for the sake of finding a new critical platform from which to speak. There are several fascinating questions to ask. For example, Why do the first reviewers barely mention the social context of the novel's release? The late 1950s and early 1960s were a time of great changes, adjusting to life after World War II and the beginnings of the civil rights movement, among many other things. So why do early reviewers not seem to be reading the novel in that context? It is also interesting to note that much criticism of the novel is by lawyers rather than literary scholars. Why? Certainly there are many books with lawyers as characters that have not attracted the attention of the legal profession in such a way.

4. **Popularity:** How is it that a novel that has been so controversial, written by a woman who shuns the spotlight, has become and remained so popular?

We know that "One year after its publication in 1960, it had gone through 500,000 copies and had been translated into ten languages. . . . In an 80-year period, from 1895 to 1975, TKM was the seventh best-selling book in the nation, and the third best-selling novel. By 1975, 11,113,909 copies of the book had been sold, and by 1982, over 15,000,000" (Johnson 13). What is it about this book that has captured readers' imaginations for 50 years?

5. **The canon:** Is *To Kill a Mockingbird* officially considered part of the literary canon? Why or why not?

The literary canon is the collection of literature considered influential in shaping culture. There can be a cyclical or reciprocal relationship between the creation of the canon and the literature most often taught in schools. Is the work taught in schools because it is in the canon, or is the work in the canon because it is most often taught in schools? It is clear that the novel was immediately taught in schools, because "since its publication in 1960, the novel has appeared on secondary school reading lists as often as any other book in English. . . . *To Kill a Mockingbird* is the fourth most frequently required book in secondary schools" (Johnson 14). Five thousand respondents to a 1991 "Survey of Lifetime Reading Habits" said that *To Kill a Mockingbird* "was second only to the Bible in being 'most often cited as making a difference'" (Johnson 14). Does this indicate that the novel is influential in shaping culture? Why or why not?

Bibliography for How to Write about *To Kill a Mockingbird*

Lee, Harper. *To Kill a Mockingbird*. 1960. New York: Harper Perennial Modern Classics, 2006. Print.

Shields, Charles J. *I Am Scout: The Biography of Harper Lee*. New York: Henry Holt and Company, 2008.

———. *Mockingbird: A Portrait of Harper Lee*. New York: Holt Paperbacks, 2007.

THEMES

READING TO WRITE

The best-known and most widely discussed themes in *To Kill a Mocking-bird* center on some aspect of race. The novel is often viewed as championing civil rights, written before the civil rights movement had found its strongest voices. Certainly the book covers race-related themes: tolerance, victimization, education, civic duty, and others. In the context of early twentieth-century Maycomb and the specific instance of Tom Robinson's trial, it seems that nearly all possible themes in *To Kill a Mockingbird* become tied to race. If this is true, then a follow-up question seems necessary: To what extent are such themes still relevant in the twenty-first century? American society is no longer struggling to reconcile formal "separate but equal" laws. Isaac Saney writes that *To Kill a Mockingbird*'s "motifs have long since outlived any positive and progressive purpose and are not only useless for today's task of building a society based on true equality, but, indeed, are a detriment and a retrogressive block" (103). So perhaps these themes are not only outdated but actually harmful?

There is much to be said about various themes, race related or not, in Harper Lee's work. As you read the following excerpt, think about the issues that surface here and punctuate the rest of the novel:

Inside the house lived a malevolent phantom. People said that he existed, but Jem and I had never seen him. People said he went out at night when the moon was down, and peeped in windows. When people's azaleas froze in a cold snap, it was because he had breathed on them. Any stealthy small crimes committed in Maycomb were his work. Once the town was terrorized by a series of morbid nocturnal events: people's chickens and household pets were found mutilated; although the culprit was Crazy Addie, who eventually drowned himself in Barker's Eddy, people still looked at the Radley Place, unwilling to discard their initial suspicions. A Negro would not pass the Radley Place at night, he would cut across to the sidewalk opposite and whistle as he walked. The Maycomb school grounds adjoined the back of the Radley lot; from the Radley chickenyard tall pecan trees shook their fruit into the schoolyard, but the nuts lay untouched by the children: Radley pecans would kill you. A baseball hit into the Radley yard was a lost ball and no questions asked.

The misery of that house began many years before Jem and I were born. The Radleys, welcome anywhere in town, kept to themselves, a predilection unforgivable in Maycomb. They did not go to church, Maycomb's principal recreation, but worshiped at home; Mrs. Radley seldom if ever crossed the street for a mid-morning coffee break with her neighbors, and certainly never joined a missionary circle. Mr. Radley walked to town at eleven-thirty every morning and came back promptly at twelve, sometimes carrying a brown paper bag that the neighborhood assumed contained the family groceries. I never knew how old Mr. Radley made his living—Jem said he 'bought cotton,' a polite term for doing nothing—but Mr. Radley and his wife had lived there with their two sons as long as anybody could remember.

The shutters and doors of the Radley house were closed on Sundays, another thing alien to Maycomb's ways: closed doors meant illness and cold weather only. Of all days Sunday was the day for formal afternoon visiting: ladies wore corsets, men wore coats, children wore shoes. But to climb the Radley front steps and call, 'He-y,' of a Sunday afternoon was something their neighbors never did. (Lee 9–10)

There is a developing theme of victimization suggested by the passage. However, the reader must determine who is the victim and who is being victimized? In this passage it seems that Boo is responsible for the town being "terrorized by a series of morbid nocturnal events," but even by the end of the excerpt, a particular tone of sadness seeps in, and readers begin to sympathize a bit for the "misery of" the Radley house.

Tolerance is another theme that announces its presence in this passage. We find clues in these few paragraphs as to how the townpeople of Maycomb treat those perceived as different, whether they do it out of fear or feel they are only being polite. Does anyone in town, in the course of the novel, reach out to the Radleys? Had anyone tried to "climb the Radley front steps and call, 'He-y'"? Even Atticus keeps his distance and seems to want the children to do the same. Calpurnia is one of the only people we see approach the Radley house of her own free will, when she runs over to warn them about the mad dog coming down the road. What does this reveal about tolerance and boundaries (physical or otherwise) throughout the book?

Think about the particular feeling or mood that you take away from the book as a whole and from select passages. What is it about the writing as well as the content that helps to create such a mood? Find particular words and phrases that support your ideas, and remember that, when you are talking about themes, you need to demonstrate that the theme encompasses the entire book or at least large portions of the book in order to establish its validity as an overarching and purposeful theme.

STRATEGIES

This section of the chapter addresses various possible topics for writing about themes in *To Kill a Mockingbird* as well as general methods for approaching these topics. These lists are in no way exhaustive and are meant to provide a jumping off point rather than an answer key. All the topics discussed in this chapter could turn into very effective papers, but use these suggestions to find your own ideas and form your own analyses.

Themes

A theme in a literary work is an idea, an action, an occurrence, or a system that in some way threads itself throughout the book. Themes are often identifiable through a close reading of words, phrases, ideas, and even chapter titles, and they are recognizable as something about which the character(s) and/or author appear to have much to say. In other words, if a book's action and/or characters continually return to a similar idea, you have probably identified a theme of the book. You can note a theme by looking for an idea or subject that informs or develops over much of a work or is repeated in some fashion throughout. It is not enough, however, merely to identify a theme. You must then interpret and analyze the theme as well as the author's treatment of it. A novel can have any number of themes, so when you are writing your essay it is usually important to focus on only one.

Sample Topics:

1. **Tolerance:** What message does Lee seem to be sending about tolerance? Is her message specific to Maycomb, or does it apply to the wider world?

   Some of the clearest examples of Lee's tolerance theme can be found in the passages describing intolerance. How does Lee want us to feel about Bob Ewell or the men who head to Tom Robinson's jail cell in the middle of the night on their mysterious errand? How can we tell that Lee wants us to feel a particular way about these characters and their actions? Is Lee's tolerance theme solely promoting tolerance of all people all of the time, or is she selective as to who deserves it? For example, if it seems clear that Lee wants readers to understand that race is not a reason for discrimination, it is equally clear that class is not a reason for intolerance, or do Lee and her characters show their bias against certain classes?

2. **Justice:** Is justice in its purest form ever found in *To Kill a Mockingbird*, or is it always tainted with compromise, sacrifice, or defeat?

   Atticus, in particular, displays a certain amount of resignation about the way things are in the American South. He knows he will not win Tom Robinson's trial, which tends to make other characters as well as readers respect him even more for doing what is morally and ethically right, despite the outcome, rather than expecting personal glory or adulation. Yet what sort of message about justice is Lee conveying with the line,

"'They've done it before and they did it tonight and they'll do it again and when they do it—seems that only children weep'" (Lee 243).

3. **Racial prejudice:** Do race issues appear throughout the novel or just in sections?

If we assume that Lee speaks through Atticus at times, you would think that she could not make her stance on race any clearer than when Atticus tells Jem:

> The one place where a man ought to get a square deal is in a courtroom, be he any color of the rainbow, but people have a way of carrying their resentments right into a jury box. As you grow older, you'll see white men cheat black men every day of your life, but let me tell you something and don't you forget it—whenever a white man does that to a black man, no matter who he is, how rich he is, or how fine a family he comes from, that white man is trash. (252)

Yet there have been a variety of interpretations of the theme of racial prejudice in *To Kill a Mockingbird.* Isaac Saney claims that black people in the novel "are robbed of their role as subjects of history, reduced to mere objects who are passive hapless victims; mere spectators and bystanders in the struggle against their own oppression and exploitation" (Saney 102). Do you find either of these themes prevalent in *To Kill a Mockingbird,* or is there yet another that you feel is even stronger? To what extent does the novel uphold racial prejudice and stereotype, even when Lee's intent seems to be the opposite? How can we interpret Scout's revelation that "Naw, Jem, I think there's just one kind of folks. Folks'" (Lee 259). Is this a firm pronouncement that all humans are equal, or does it unnecessarily (if innocently perhaps) erase some of the differences between people that make us interesting, unique, individualized human beings?

4. **Courage:** In what ways is courage defined in the novel?

How does Harper Lee define courage? How do the various characters define it? If courage is associated with literary heroes, is there more than one hero in the novel? Whose courage is more important, or pervasive, or relevant to today's readers? The character who seems most obviously courageous is Atticus, and yet when he speaks to Jem of courage, he is talking about Mrs. Dubose: "'I wanted you to see something about her—I wanted you to see what real courage is, instead of getting the idea that courage is a man with a gun in his hand. It's when you know you're licked before you begin but you begin anyway and you see it through no matter what'" (Lee 128). In this passage, Atticus clearly describes himself, though he does not seem to recognize that fact. Is he also describing Tom Robinson? Boo Radley?

5. **Sympathy/empathy:** Is there a clear difference between sympathy and empathy throughout the novel? If so, is one generally considered better than the other?

Who is the most empathetic character in the book, and in what ways does this quality harm or help him or her? Is Atticus the best example of an empathetic character, or does he only empathize with certain other characters, rather than everyone? For whom do readers feel sympathy? Why? Does Lee seem to want us to sympathize with these characters? How can we tell? What is Lee's larger, overriding message about sympathy and empathy?

6. **Social status/caste system:** What role does social status or class play in the novel?

Readers can find clear delineations between the Ewells and other, better-off characters in the novel. Are the Ewells (Bob Ewell, in particular) villainized at least partly because of their social/financial status? Such prejudice often goes unnoticed or unremarked on because it is so ingrained in the characters that even they do not recognize it. The following passage seems fairly innocent until you start thinking about the possible implications of such labels, assumptions, and generalizations:

> There was indeed a caste system in Maycomb, but to my mind it worked this way: the old citizens, the present generation of people who had lived side by side for years and years, were utterly predictable to one another: they took for granted attitudes, character shadings, even gestures, as having been repeated in each generation and refined by time. Thus the dicta No Crawford Minds His Own Business, Every Third Merriweather is Morbid, The Truth Is Not in the Delafields, All the Bufords Walk Like That, were simply guides to daily living. (Lee 149)

Does this passage help us to understand what happened to the Radleys? The Ewells? Should we be more skeptical of the Finch family's standing in the community, assuming that they are respected at least partly because of their background and status rather than their own intelligence or humanity?

7. **Education:** What is the role of education in *To Kill a Mockingbird*? How important is it to each character? Why?

How does each character define "a good education" or "an educated person"? Why? What does this reveal about these characters or about Harper Lee's own views? How can you tell? There is a major discrepancy in regard to education in the book: "the education motif—far from being incidental—is a center for the ironic contrast between what is 'taught' and what is 'learned,' a contrast that lies at the very heart of the novel" (Schuster 507). We can see that Scout learns a lot by the end of the novel and certainly even more by the time she is an adult looking back on these years in Maycomb. How much of what she knows has been specifically taught to her, and how much of it is what she learns through other means? Why is the distinction between what is taught and what is learned so important?

8. **Superstition:** Which characters in the novel are superstitious? Why? About what?

In what ways is superstition linked to race? Why? How does this affect Scout, Dill, and Jem? Calpurnia is one of the first to point out the racial divide in superstition to the children. Jem describes Hot Steams to Dill, and Scout says, "Don't believe a word he says, Dill. . . . Calpurnia says that's nigger-talk" (Lee 41). Why would Calpurnia say this? What does it reveal about her own views or possibly Harper Lee's views? To what extent are superstitions tied to race? Why? Are racial issues at least partly an extension of superstitions about other groups of people?

Bibliography for Themes

Lee, Harper. *To Kill a Mockingbird.* 1960. New York: Harper Perennial Modern Classics, 2006. Print.

Saney, Isaac. "Commentary: The Case Against *To Kill a Mockingbird.*" *Race and Class* vol. 45 (1): 99–110.

Schuster, Edgar H. "Discovering Theme and Structure in the Novel." *The English Journal* no. 7, vol. 52 (October 1963): 506–11.

CHARACTERS

READING TO WRITE

To Kill a Mockingbird is certainly a character-driven novel. There are important plot elements, as well, but, in assessing and discussing the novel, it is crucial that readers get to know the characters and feel close to them. It is interesting to read the novel while trying to figure out which characters Lee seems to want us to feel particularly close to. It is also interesting to ask whether there are any characters that seem extraneous to the book or if each character has a particular role or function that helps move the book along.

A reporter once asked Harper Lee: "Were the characters in the book based on real people?" Harper Lee answered: "No, but the people at home think so. The beauty of it, though, is that no two people come up with the same identification. They never think of themselves as being portrayed in the book. They try to identify others whom they know as characters" (qtd. in Shields *Mockingbird* 223). Certainly there are (or were) people who specifically identified characters as people they knew. Can we do the same thing, even though many years have passed since these characters would have actually lived? If you feel you particularly relate to a character or characters, go back and investigate the way that Harper Lee writes that character to see if you can figure out why and how you relate so well. Is this Lee's intent? How can you tell?

Harper Lee often gives fairly brief initial introductions to characters, sometimes allowing the full characterization to emerge from others' reactions to and discussions about the character: "Mrs. Dubose was plain hell" (Lee 7). This type of incredibly brief description sets readers up to want to know more. It gives a brief but extremely accurate and compelling description of characters or at least elements of characters with which Scout would be familiar. We have to remember that, regardless of who is saying what about whom, all of the information is filtered through Scout's mind, whether it is her mind as a child or as an adult.

Arguably the most compelling bit of characterization in the novel comes near the end:

> He was still leaning against the wall. He had been leaning against the wall when I came into the room, his arms folded across his chest. As I pointed he brought his arms down and pressed the palms of his hands against the wall. They were white hands, sickly white hands that had never seen the sun, so white they stood out garishly against the dull cream wall in the dim light of Jem's room.
>
> I looked from his hands to his sand-stained khaki pants; my eyes traveled up his thin frame to his torn denim shirt. His face was as white as his hands, but for a shadow on his jutting chin. His cheeks were thin to hollowness; his mouth was wide; there were shallow, almost delicate indentations at his temples, and his gray eyes were so colorless I thought he was blind. His hair was dead and thin, almost feathery on top of his head.
>
> When I pointed to him his palms slipped slightly, leaving greasy sweat streaks on the wall, and he hooked his thumbs in his belt. A strange small spasm shook him, as if he heard fingernails scrape slate, but as I gazed at him in wonder the tension slowly drained from his face. His lips parted into a timid smile, and our neighbor's image blurred with my sudden tears.
>
> 'Hey, Boo,' I said. (Lee 310)

Most of this is simply a physical description of Boo Radley. Do readers know or guess that it is Boo before Scout uses his name? How so? Is this what Lee intended? Why is the physical description of Boo so important for an understanding of his character? What does each detail about Boo reveal about who he is and what he is like? Is it fair for us, for Scout, for Lee to come to conclusions about Boo based on these observations, rather than long conversations with him? Why or why not?

These questions and others like them can help you to delve deeply into the characterizations contained in *To Kill a Mockingbird*.

STRATEGIES

This section of the chapter addresses various possible topics for writing about characters in *To Kill a Mockingbird* as well as general methods for approaching these topics. These lists are in no way exhaustive and are meant to provide a jumping off point rather than an answer key. Use these suggestions to find your own ideas and form your own analyses.

Characters

Writing about character allows you to choose one person from the novel to study in great detail. You can investigate how Lee differentiates between characters. How, for example, does she help readers form immediate distinctions between Scout and Jem? These two characters could easily have turned out to be similar to each other, but Lee instead makes readers see and feel different things about each child. What effects do these differences have on readers? Are we more sympathetic to Scout or to Jem? What is it about these characters that creates such impressions and emotions? The characters in *To Kill a Mockingbird* are some of the best-known characters in all of literature. Why do you suppose that these particular characters are so memorable?

Characters can be written about in several different ways, including character development (such as how Scout changes or remains the same throughout the work), methods of characterization (such as what we learn about Scout through her own revelations versus what we learn about her through others' comments, behavior, and observations), and even how we determine who is a character and who is not (in this case, we can ask whether or not the South should be considered a character and why or why not). Many of the categories in this book overlap, allowing one observation to lead to a more complex understanding of the novel's various elements and how they are interconnected. For example, noting the prevalence of children as characters in *To Kill a Mockingbird* might lead you to discover a particular theme in the work as well.

When you write about character, you need to determine how we as readers get to know the characters in the story. The ways in which an author reveals or leaks information about a character can be as important as the characterization itself. Do we learn the most about Atticus through his own words? Through his actions? Through the other characters' reactions to him or conversations about him? How does Lee make her characters seem so real to us? It is important to look at character in terms of broad strokes like which specific actions certain characters take, but it is equally important to study the methods of characterization that are easy to overlook: a character's manner of speaking, the images or setting connected with a character, the repetition of words and phrases associated with a character, other characters' reactions to and discussions about a character, and the narrator's (and/or author's) commentary on a character. Lee's characterizations in the novel can be complex and subtle, making a second reading even more entertaining and full of discovery.

There are many questions to ask that will get you started on an essay topic: How does Lee help signal readers as to when they should like a character (or feel sorry for him/her) and when they should distrust a character? Are the characters ordinary, or do they just seem so on the surface or in the eyes of other characters? Do people today read too much through a twenty-first-century lens, unable to see how progressive the novel was for its time? Do we no longer see Atticus as the same level of hero simply because, forty years later, he does not go far enough?

You might also respond to scholars and reviewers who have written about the novel. Elizabeth Lee Haselden, for example, writes, "This is a good book, not a great one; an interesting book, but not a compelling one. . . . The book offers no character with whom the reader can identify himself, depicts on the part of no one involved in the trial any inner struggle for an ethical answer to injustice, and is lacking in real compassion for people" (29). Do you agree? Why or why not? What evidence is in the book to support these arguments?

Sample topics:

1. **The Radleys:** Why are the Radleys as an entire family so important in the novel?

   It seems that we get to know the entire Radley family as a whole, rather than learning about each individual member, as we do with other characters. Why is it important to see the Radleys as a group? Who comments on the Radleys, and who refuses to share an opinion about the family? Why is this significant? Think about what Calpurnia says in front of the children when she sees Mr. Radley: "'There goes the meanest man ever God blew breath into,' murmured Calpurnia, and she spat meditatively into the yard. We looked at her in surprise, for Calpurnia rarely commented on the ways of white people" (Lee 13). Is Mr. Radley so despicable that even Calpurnia will break her own pattern in order to mutter something hateful about him? Or might there be other reasons for her comments? How does Calpurnia's comment (and Scout's explanation following it) help to show how Lee wants us to feel about Mr. Radley?

2. **Boo Radley:** Is Boo Radley one of the heroes of the novel? Why or why not?

How do you feel about Boo Radley after Scout recounts the story of his father keeping him in the house? What about after hearing that he stuck scissors into his father's leg? How does Lee want us to feel about Boo at this point, and how can you tell? We finally get a detailed description of Boo when Scout gets to see him at the end of the novel. What effect does the description as well as its placement in the novel have on Lee's characterization of Boo as well as our reactions to him? How heavily do readers rely on Scout's reaction to Boo to inform us of his true nature? Think about the following statements made by Thomas Mallon, and consider what they argue about Lee's writing as well as Boo's role in the novel: "Boo Radley, the agonized recluse living just down the street from the Finches, remains hidden and tantalizing for most of the novel, almost like the authorial imagination that never quite frees itself from fine sentiment. But in the end Boo, too, is there to do good; once he's done it, Scout takes him by the hand and leads him out of the book" (81). Do you agree with Mallon? Why or why not?

3. **Miss Maudie Atkinson:** Miss Maudie is a neighbor, but she seems to fulfill several roles: mother, friend, vessel of information. In what ways is Miss Maudie's character important to the novel?

Is Miss Maudie the most insightful, the character best able to really see the world around her as it really is? She is critical of the world, yet she resides within it with grace and, sometimes, resignation, only allowing certain people to hear her more pointed comments. How does she earn the children's trust, and why is this so critical to their relationship as well as the novel as a whole? Why does Miss Maudie seem to understand Atticus so well?

4. **The Ewells:** Are there any redeeming qualities about the Ewells?

How does Lee seem to want readers to feel about the Ewells? Why? How can you tell? Are the Ewells an example of pure malevolence, or are there gray areas? Why are the Ewells so often compared with animals? How does this relate to race issues in the novel? Can we make comparisons between the Ewells and the Cunninghams? Why or why not? Do we know the Ewells as a family unit or as individuals? Why is this important?

5. **Atticus Finch:** Is Atticus the heart of the novel?

Is Atticus a hero, or does he not go far enough? Why could he not prevent the court from being so unfair? Did he try hard enough? The epigraph, or quotation that opens a novel, seems to place Atticus at the center: "Lawyers, I suppose, were children once." What does this quotation and its placement in the book reveal about the novel? About Atticus? One description of Atticus notes: "He liked Maycomb, he was Maycomb County born and bred; he knew his people, they knew him, and because of Simon Finch's industry, Atticus was related by blood or marriage to nearly every family in the town" (Lee 5). Does this lend credence to Atticus's opinions later in the novel, when he says that the trial will not really change anything, that people are not ready? Does it set him up as a trustworthy spokesperson for the town? Does it demonstrate how thorough his defiance must have been when protecting and defending Tom Robinson, because he would have known exactly how the town would react? Is Atticus a realist, a pessimist, or something in between? He tells Scout that he will not win Tom Robinson's case; "'Just because we were licked a hundred years before we started is no reason for us not to try to win'" (Lee 87). Is he an optimist of some kind?

What are Atticus's qualities as a father? How do the children view him, and what comments do they make specifically about his parenting? Are these qualities generally acceptable in a father? Do you think Atticus was really detached, or is that just Scout's perspective? If he was detached, why? If not, why would Scout see it that way?

One of the most memorable things about Atticus is the respect shown for him by various people, particularly the black people in the courtroom. Does this respect help readers distinguish between likeable and unlikeable characters? Those who show respect for Atticus are automatically likeable, in other words?

6. **The South:** Is the South a character? How does Lee define or characterize it?

For what reasons might it be important to view the South as a character? Do you think Lee sees the South as a character, a setting, both, or neither? Why? How is information about the South revealed to us? Why is this significant? What do characters' reactions to the South reveal about them? In what ways would the novel have to change if the South were not such a big part? Would these changes make the novel more effective or less?

7. **Aunt Alexandra:** What is Aunt Alexandra's role in the novel? In the family? How well does she fulfill these roles?

To what extent do we obtain information about Aunt Alexandra from other people's opinions of her? Why is this important? Does she represent the other white townspeople in terms of her opinions on race? Is she really just worried about her family? Does she turn out to be so bad after all? Many of her fears actually come true (or almost come true). Is she modeled on Harper Lee's mother? What might this change about our reading of her character? Does Aunt Alexandra represent the woman Scout will (or should) grow up to be? Why or why not? What is Atticus's attitude toward his sister? How does this shape our opinions of both Atticus and Aunt Alexandra?

8. **Jem Finch:** What about Jem? Is this his coming-of-age story too?

Is Jem the real hero of the novel? The story begins and ends with him after all. Scout thinks her brother is a hero: "Jem was a born hero" (Lee 44). Is this true only in the context of their Radley melodrama or only because Scout admires her older brother? Is it true in a larger or different context as well? Jem wants to be a gentleman like Atticus, but he tears Mrs. Dubose's yard apart. What sets him off? Is this a heroic act? To what extent does Jem really feel responsible for Scout? How can you tell? Is Jem sometimes more of a parental figure than Atticus? How so? Why or why not?

9. **Jean Louise "Scout" Finch:** Is Scout the hero? The protagonist? Or is she just the vessel through with information is disseminated to readers?

How can we tell which of Scout's observations/opinions are innocent remarks from a child and which are scathing indictments from an adult looking back at her youth? Why is it so important to distinguish between young Scout and adult Jean Louise? How does Scout see herself? Why? Do her observations and insights reveal more about other characters or about herself? How so? Discussion of education and reading materials early in the novel set Scout up as precocious, so we know not to expect typical six-year-old thoughts, information, and ideas. Do we believe that such a small child could be this observant, insightful, and wise? Why or why not? How does Harper Lee want us to feel about Scout? How can you tell?

10. **Calpurnia:** Does Calpurnia help us understand race issues in the novel? How?

Is Calpurnia a better parent than Atticus? Than Aunt Alexandra? Why or why not? What is Calpurnia's role in the novel? In the Finch family? How is she viewed differently by white people and black people? Why? Is Calpurnia the children's protector, above all else, or are they in some ways protecting her? Does Calpurnia's place in the Finch household contradict the family's views on race in general? What does Calpurnia's character teach us about class issues as well as race issues?

Bibliography for Characters

Haselden, Elizabeth Lee. "*To Kill a Mockingbird* Lacks Realistic Characters." O'Neill, Terry, ed. *Readings on To Kill a Mockingbird.* Literary Companion Series. San Diego: Greenhaven Press, 2000. 29–31.

Lee, Harper. *To Kill a Mockingbird.* 1960. New York: Harper Perennial Modern Classics, 2006. Print.

Shields, Charles J. *I Am Scout: The Biography of Harper Lee.* New York: Henry Holt and Company, 2008.

———. *Mockingbird: A Portrait of Harper Lee.* New York: Holt Paperbacks, 2007.

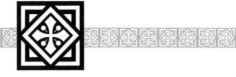

FORM AND GENRE

READING TO WRITE

Part one of *To Kill a Mockingbird* ends with the following paragraphs:

> "She was. She had her own views about things, a lot different from mine, maybe . . . son, I told you that if you hadn't lost your head I'd have made you go read to her. I wanted you to see something about her—I wanted you to see what real courage is, instead of getting the idea that courage is a man with a gun in his hand. It's when you know you're licked before you begin but you begin anyway and you see it through no matter what. You rarely win, but sometimes you do. Mrs. Dubose won, all ninety-eight pounds of her. According to her views, she died beholden to nothing and nobody. She was the bravest person I ever knew."
>
> Jem picked up the candy box and threw it in the fire. He picked up the camellia, and when I went off to bed I saw him fingering the wide petals. Atticus was reading the paper.

How does this help pull part one together, perhaps in regard to a particular theme, point of view, or idea? Do we get a sense that something is ending here or that something is beginning? Why? Why do you think Lee chose to end this section of the novel at this specific point and identify it as part one? What does part one have in common that part two does not? Part two of *To Kill a Mockingbird* begins with the following paragraphs:

> Jem was twelve. He was difficult to live with, inconsistent, moody. His appetite was appalling, and he told me so many times to stop pestering

him I consulted Atticus: "Reckon he's got a tapeworm?" Atticus said no, Jem was growing. I must be patient with him and disturb him as little as possible.

This change in Jem had come about in a matter of weeks. Mrs. Dubose was not cold in her grave—Jem had seemed grateful enough for my company when he went to read to her. Overnight, it seemed, Jem had required an alien set of values and was trying to impose them on me: several times he went so far as to tell me what to do. After one altercation when Jem hollered, "It's time you started bein' a girl and acting right!" I burst into tears and fled to Calpurnia.

Thus, part two seems to take up just where part one left off. Why, then, the division between them? What does part two have in common with the remainder of the novel that part one does not? Is the tone of each part the same? How so?

STRATEGIES

This section of the chapter addresses various possible topics for writing about the form and genre of *To Kill a Mockingbird* as well as general methods for approaching these topics. These lists are in no way exhaustive and are meant to provide a jumping off point rather than an answer key. Use these suggestions to find your own ideas and form your own analyses.

Form and Genre

Form and genre provide ways of classifying works that allow us to study them more fully. Form is defined as the style and structure of a work, whereas genre is the type, or classification, of a work. Both form and genre are usually distinct from a work's content, though writers use each element specifically in order to convey a particular message, reach a certain audience, or to simply strengthen the impact of their work.

Harper Lee's editors and friends say that initially *To Kill a Mockingbird* read like a series of stories rather than a cohesive novel, making Lee's revision process fairly intensive: "For Nelle, it was like assembling puzzle pieces of scenes and short stories into a narrative whole" (Shields *Mockingbird* 130). Is any of this process still evident in the novel? Sometimes, for example, it might seem like there is a lack of transition between paragraphs or chapters. Is this a flaw, or an element of Lee's writing style to be celebrated?

Sometimes gender, religion, race, or other factors can play a role in a writer's choices concerning form and genre. One scholar writes that "Miss Lee does write like a woman. She paints Scout in warm tones, and we like the child" (Bruell 659). What does this mean exactly? Could a man have written the same book? Why or why not? What would be different? The same?

Sample Topics:

1. **Coming-of-age story:** Is there more than one coming-of-age story in *To Kill a Mockingbird*?

   A coming-of-age story can also be called a *bildungsroman,* a term often associated with Lee's novel. Clearly this is Scout's story of growing up in Maycomb, Alabama. The entire novel takes its shape from her split child/adult perspectives and is framed around her learning process as she grows older and presumably wiser. What rites of passage is Scout subjected to? How effective are they in helping to move the novel's action along? Are there other characters whose coming-of-age process helps to frame the novel? Which elements of Scout's growing process (or Scout herself) are integral to the entire novel?

2. **Southern gothic fiction:** In what ways is *To Kill a Mockingbird* a southern novel? Does it reflect the generic elements associated with southern gothic writing?

   Consider which of the following characteristics of southern gothic fiction are present in *To Kill a Mockingbird:*

   > murders, ghosts, witches, werewolves, vampires, monsters, imprisonment, ruins, nostalgia for the past, unnatural parents, haunted or decayed quarters, specters, forebodings, deformity, madness, magic, dark and forbidding secrets, sexual violence,

rape, incest, insanity, mental breakdown, and cultural decay. (Johnson 40)

Clearly it is not necessary to include every single one of these characteristics in order to qualify as southern gothic fiction. How many of them are present or suggested in *To Kill a Mockingbird*? Does the combination qualify the novel to call itself southern gothic? To what degree are Lee's southern roots as well as the Alabama setting integral to the novel? How would the novel change if its setting were changed?

3. **Point of view:** Why are there two points of view in the novel?

There is a lot of debate about Scout's voice in *To Kill a Mockingbird*. Some scholars claim that the split between Scout's child voice and her adult voice is distracting and clunky, while others argue that this is perhaps the most effective element in the novel. Harper Lee herself had some trouble figuring out the narrative voice:

> It might be that Lee floundered when she was trying to settle on a point of view. She rewrote the novel three times: the original draft was in the third person, then she changed to the first person and later rewrote the final draft, which blended the two narrators, Janus-like, looking forward and back at the same time. She later called this a 'hopeless period' of writing the novel over and over. (Shields *Mockingbird* 128)

Were her efforts worth all of that trouble? Do these duel voices of Scout overshadow other characters' voices, or can we still in some ways hear Boo, Tom, Atticus, and others?

4. **Part one and part two:** What are the distinctions between parts one and two?

Why does Lee divide the book as she does? What would change if she had left it as one continuous narrative instead of dividing it into two parts? Can each part of the novel be clearly characterized, distinct from the other part? What effects would it have if Lee divided the novel into more than two parts?

5. **Parallelism/cyclical structure:** Does the parallelism between the beginning and ending help readers to feel a sense of closure?

The narrative essentially begins at the end and then takes readers back through the events that led up to Jem getting his arm broken. Does this make the entire book a flashback? What effect does this have on the narration? Does it help justify the presence of the dual voices, young Scout and older Scout, in the novel?

6. **Film:** Does watching the film help us to better understand the novel?

There are several key differences between the film and the novel versions of *To Kill a Mockingbird.* Horton Foote wrote the screenplay, but Harper Lee enthusiastically supported the film: "'If the integrity of a film adaptation is measured by the degree to which the novelist's intent is preserved, Mr. Foote's screenplay should be studied as a classic'" (Shields *Mockingbird* 206). Has the film become an integral part of the *To Kill a Mockingbird* experience, more so even than other books that have been made into films? Why or why not? Is this helpful, or does it distract from the book and the experience of reading it and leave less to the imagination?

Bibliography for Form and Genre

Bruell, Edwin. "Keen Scalpel on Racial Ills." *English Journal,* vol. 53, no. 9 (December 1964): 658–61.

Johnson, Claudia Durst. *Understanding To Kill a Mockingbird: A Student Casebook to Issues, Sources, and Historic Documents.* Westport, Conn.: Greenwood Press, 1994.

Lee, Harper. *To Kill a Mockingbird.* 1960. New York: Harper Perennial Modern Classics, 2006. Print.

Shields, Charles J. *I Am Scout: The Biography of Harper Lee.* New York: Henry Holt and Company, 2008.

————. *Mockingbird: A Portrait of Harper Lee.* New York: Holt Paperbacks, 2007.

LANGUAGE, SYMBOLS, AND IMAGERY

READING TO WRITE

Reading a novel for clues about language, symbols, and imagery can be like putting together a puzzle. You know that all of the pieces are there, and now you need to find ways in which they fit together. Meaning is created, interpreted, and understood in the way you assemble the pieces into a unified vision of the whole.

Consider the following brief passage from early in the novel:

For reasons unfathomable to the most experienced prophets in Maycomb County, autumn turned to winter that year. We had two weeks of the coldest weather since 1885, Atticus said. Mr. Avery said it was written on the Rosetta Stone that when children disobeyed their parents, smoked cigarettes and made war on each other, the seasons would change: Jem and I were burdened with the guilt of contributing to the aberrations of nature, thereby causing unhappiness to our neighbors and discomfort to ourselves.

Old Mrs. Radley died that winter, but her death caused hardly a ripple—the neighborhood seldom saw her, except when she watered her cannas. Jem and I decided that Boo had got her at last, but when Atticus returned home from the Radley house he said she died of natural causes, to our disappointment. (Lee 72)

This passage seems to reveal much about the things that are out of the characters' control. Consider how various characters react when they find something out of their control. What do their reactions reveal about them? How do various characters respond specifically to the changing seasons and weather? Why is this important?

Weather and seasons play a significant role in *To Kill a Mockingbird.* Why do you think Lee brings winter to Maycomb, and why is it particularly important that Alabama rarely sees snow but receives some in this particular year? How would we read the book, or these chapters, differently if they were set in a place that receives snow regularly?

In the first sentence of this passage, which is the first sentence of chapter eight, Scout uses the word *prophet* to refer to some people in Maycomb. Why? What does the word mean, and what might it symbolize here? Is Scout (or Lee) being facetious, making fun of Maycomb residents a little bit, or is their description as prophets considered an accurate one? How can we tell?

What is the significance of Mr. Avery in this passage and this chapter? In what ways does he become a symbol or become symbolized by something else? We might ask ourselves whether Mr. Avery really referred to the Rosetta Stone or if that is a misinterpretation, a mishearing, by the children. Why would either be significant? What is the Rosetta Stone, and what does it represent? Does it represent the same things or types of things in the novel?

In this passage, the weather becomes a symbolic representation of children's behavior. To what extent do people in Maycomb appear to believe these associations, and to what extent is this Mr. Avery's strange perception? If things as inconstant as the weather become symbolic of children's naughtiness, what sort of burden does that place on children? Does this use of symbolism lead to any thoughts about a theme in the book or chapter?

Is it important that Mrs. Radley dies in the winter, as opposed to any of the other seasons? Why? Scout says that "her death caused hardly a ripple," which suggests the town is a body of water whose surface could be disturbed. Is there other water imagery or symbolism in the novel? Does this instance mean that the people in the town move and think as if they are in or under water? Does this lead to any "sink or swim" types of clichés?

STRATEGIES

This section of the chapter addresses various possible topics for writing about the language, symbols, and imagery of *To Kill a Mockingbird* as well as general methods for approaching these topics. These lists are in no way exhaustive and are meant to provide a jumping-off point rather than an answer key. Use these suggestions to find your own ideas and form your own analyses. All topics discussed in this chapter could lead to strong, original essays.

Language, Symbols, and Imagery

Literary works are studied not only for their content but for their style as well. This requires you to avoid summarizing the text unnecessarily and focus instead on the way in which the work was written. It no longer concerns what the work is about but rather how it is constructed and conveyed. Studying the language of a text allows you to look carefully at elements such as syntax, word choice, and diction. You might, for example, study the various accents, dialects, and colloquialisms used and expressed by characters in *To Kill a Mockingbird* to help you delve more deeply into Lee's characterizations. What does a character's use of language reveal about him or her? Language might also mean a search into the words most commonly used to describe a character, a setting, or an activity. Look at the tone (or mood) surrounding Scout and Jem, for example, and pinpoint elements of language that help to create that tone. Then take it a step further by discussing why it is significant that such a mood is connected with these particular characters.

Writing about the language, symbols, and imagery within a novel requires you to look specifically at how the work is constructed, as opposed to just studying the content of the work. Pay particular attention to words, phrases, and the repetition of words, phrases and ideas in order to begin to see how Lee uses language, symbols, and imagery. Summarizing the content may be necessary for illustrating particular points, but it is not the end product of this type of essay. You will want to consider the words chosen, how they are arranged into sentences and paragraphs, and how they convey notions of character and theme. Do some characters speak differently from others? If so, why? Speech can be tied to any number of other elements and themes to consider, such as economic class, education, geography, and stress, just to name a few. Discovering that two characters have distinct ways of speaking might lead you to research on economic classes and their respective educations, requiring some background in the historical context. Ultimately, you are looking at Lee's choices as a writer and the possible reasons behind such choices.

Finding symbolism in a work involves looking for an object, action, or motif that stands for something else. Is a mad dog just a mad dog in *To Kill a Mockingbird*, or might it represent something entirely different? What ideas, activities, and objects preoccupy or obsess the novel and its characters? These elements might come in the form of letters or particular foods, for example, or they might be somewhat more abstract notions such as a particular color being associated with a particular theme or attitude throughout the book.

Imagery encapsulates things that can be perceived with our senses. Are there elements of imagery that recur throughout the novel, perhaps associated with specific characters, places, or activities? For example, is it always dark and dreary around a certain character, offering a clue to this character's disposition or lifestyle or the ways in which Lee is asking us to perceive this character? Harper Lee has said, "I think the thing that I most deplore about American writing, and especially in the American theater, is a lack of craftsmanship. It comes right down to this—the lack of absolute love for language, the lack of sitting down and working a good idea into a gem of an idea. It takes time and patience and effort to turn out a work of art, and few people seem willing to go all the way. . . . There's no substitute for the love of language, for the beauty of an English sentence. There's no substitute for struggling, if a struggle is needed, to make an English sentence as beautiful as it should be" (Newquist 408–09).

Like Jane Austen, Lee was "very mindful of storytelling" (Blackall 20). How is this evident in Lee's text?

Sample Topics:

1. **Reliable narrator(s):** Why do we trust (or do we?) that adult Scout remembers conversations in such great detail? Does it matter if she is getting things exactly right? Why or why not?

Do we trust Scout more when she is older or when she is younger? How can we tell the difference between the two narrators? The children hear a lot from others as well. Are we expected to trust them? How much of Miss Crawford's tales are we expected to believe? What are the indications that a narrator or speaker may not be entirely trustworthy? Two very different reviews of the novel demonstrate scholars' arguments about the novel's narration: "[T]old in the first person by a six-year-old girl with the prose style of a well-educated adult. . . . Miss Lee has, to be sure, made an attempt to confine the information in the text to what Scout would actually know, but it is no more than a casual gesture toward plausibility" (Adams). On the other hand, Richard Sullivan writes: "The unaffected young narrator uses adult language to render the matter she deals with, but the point of view is cunningly restricted to that of a perceptive, independent child, who doesn't always understand fully what's happening, but who conveys completely, by implication, the weight and burden of the story" (15). Which opinion do you agree with, and why?

2. **Metaphor:** Where in the novel does Lee use metaphor most effectively?

Consider the following interpretation: "Is not the mockingbird a metaphor for the entire African American population? . . . Black people are useful and harmless creatures—akin to decorous pets—that should not be treated brutally. . . . What it attacks are the worst—particularly violent—excesses of the racist social order, leaving the racist social order itself intact" (Saney 102). Do you agree with this reading of the metaphor surrounding the mockingbird? Such an interpretation certainly brings to light several issues in regard to race and Lee's treatment of race in the novel. If the book ultimately leaves the "racist social order itself intact," does that mean that the metaphor involving the mockingbird fails in some way or proves ineffective? Do you think this was Lee's explicit intention?

3. **Vocabulary:** In what ways is the vocabulary in the novel distinctive?

Why does Lee make the vocabulary choices that appear in the novel? How effective are they? Is the vocabulary particular to the South? The time period? Both? Consider words such as *flivver* (11), *scuppernongs* (39), *hoodooing* (67), and *touchous* (73). Is Scout's vocabulary realistic for a child her age, during this time period, with her education? How does this affect our understanding of the novel's setting and our characterizations?

4. **Mad dog as symbol:** Are there characters in the novel who are more unpredictable and dangerous than the mad dog that Atticus shoots?

Consider the following passage:

> the atmosphere in the courtroom was exactly the same as a cold February morning, when the mockingbirds were still, and the carpenters had stopped hammering on Miss Maudie's new house, and every wood door in the neighborhood was shut as tight as the doors of the Radley Place. A deserted, waiting, empty street, and the courtroom was packed with people. A steaming summer night was no different from a winter morning . . . it was like watching Atticus walk into the street, raise a rifle to his shoulder and pull the trigger, but watching all the time knowing that the gun was empty. (Lee 240)

Is Bob Ewell the mad dog? Is Tom Robinson embodied by the mad dog as well as the mockingbird?

5. **Mockingbird as symbol:** Is the mockingbird a symbol of Boo? Of Tom?

The mockingbird is perhaps the most prominent symbol in the book. What does it represent? Remember, a symbol can represent more than one thing at times. Sometimes a symbol can change throughout a book and come to represent different things at different times. Are there any situations, for example, when the children (Jem, Scout, and Dill) are the mockingbirds? At what moments in the book are characters talking or thinking specifically about mockingbirds? What makes these instances memorable and important? Why do the characters talk about the sin of killing a mockingbird, rather than just talking directly about the problems they face and the people the mockingbird represents? Is the symbolism more effective than a blatant conversation about leaving harmless people alone? Does Scout's comment about killing a mockingbird (in regard to Boo) indicate that "Southern justice fails for those who are 'different'" (May 94)? What are the larger thematic implications of the mockingbird as symbol?

6. **Snowman as symbol:** What might the snowman symbolize?

In a book that centers in many ways on race issues, it seems particularly significant that the children make a snowman out of black dirt and then cover it with white snow. How does this symbolize race in the novel? Scout says, "'Jem, I ain't ever heard of a nigger snowman'" (Lee 75). Not only does this observation draw our attention to what is now considered politically incorrect language (and what at the time would also have indicated a certain negative attitude toward black people), but it makes the point that black people remain on the fringes of society. What else might the snowman come to symbolize? Earthiness? Is it akin to someone being described as "the salt of the earth," to actually make a person out of the earth? Does it have religious or creationist significance? Why might it be important that the snowman looks like Mr. Avery? Why is Miss Maudie so upset? She says, they have "erected an absolute morphodite in that yard! Atticus, you'll never raise 'em!'" (Lee 77). In what ways does the snowman reflect Atticus's parenting style and competence?

7. **Seasons as parameters for book's events:** Why is it important to note when in the seasonal calendar that certain events take place?

What kinds of things happen in each season? Does each season develop a particular mood or expectation for readers? Literature often uses fairly standard associations with seasons: Spring, for example, is usually a time of new growth and possibility. Does Lee deviate from these standard associations with the four seasons? What impact does the Alabama setting have? Would the associations and interpretations of events look different if the action of the novel took place in a more extreme climate such as Alaska?

Early in the novel, Lee writes, "There are no clearly defined seasons in South Alabama; summer drifts into autumn, and autumn is sometimes never followed by winter, but turns to a days-old spring that melts into summer again" (Lee 67). This seems ironic or strange, since events in the book are clearly delineated by seasons. What does the phrase "sometimes never" add to this description?

Make a list of things that happen in each season, and make special note of things that happen in extreme or unusual weather. Why is it important that Miss Maudie's fire takes place in the winter, for example? What events does the fire lead to that add significance to the event and/or the season? You might also look for ways in which Lee uses the weather or seasons to describe people or events and ask yourself what it adds to the description or our interpretation when we learn that at one point Atticus's voice is "like the winter wind" (Lee 119).

8. **Left/wrong versus right/right:** How are notions of, for example, left- or righthandedness associated with notions of right and wrong, justice and morality?

Lee writes that "[Atticus] was nearly blind in his left eye, and said left eyes were the tribal curse of the Finches. Whenever he wanted to see something well, he turned his head and looked from his right eye" (102). If Atticus is regarded as the voice of reason and fairness in the novel and his path is the proverbial straight and narrow, what could it mean that he only sees well out of his right eye? Does the physical direction right equate with "correct" in some way here? Is this irony, perhaps, that Atticus sees more clearly than anyone else in the novel, even with only one good eye?

Consider also the importance of left and right (eyes and arms) during the trial. Are right and left simply equivalents of, respectively, correct/right and wrong/left in these situations? Are there other interpretations available for these occurrences?

Bibliography for Language, Symbols, and Imagery

Adams, Phoebe. Review of *To Kill a Mockingbird*. *Atlantic Monthly*, August 1960.

Lee, Harper. *To Kill a Mockingbird*. 1960. New York: Harper Perennial Modern Classics, 2006. Print.

Richard Sullivan, *Chicago Sunday Tribune* "Engrossing First Novel of Rare Excellence." 17 July 1960, p. 15.

HISTORY AND CONTEXT

READING TO WRITE

Harper Lee once wrote that "We Americans like to put our culture into disposable containers. Nowhere is this more evident than in the way we treat our past" (Lee, "Romance"). How does Lee treat the past in *To Kill a Mockingbird*? Does she seem to be putting it into a disposable container, or is she doing something entirely new and different with it? How can we tell?

Consider the following passage:

"I mean how can Hitler just put a lot of folks in a pen like that, looks like the govamint'd stop him," said the owner of the hand.

"Hitler is the government," said Miss Gates, and seizing an opportunity to make education dynamic, she went to the blackboard. She printed DEMOCRACY in large letters. "Democracy," she said. "Does anybody have a definition?"

"Us," somebody said.

I raised my hand, remembering an old campaign slogan Atticus had once told me about.

"What do you think it means, Jean Louise?"

"'Equal rights for all, special privileges for none,'" I quoted.

"Very good, Jean Louise, very good," Miss Gates smiled. In front of DEMOCRACY, she printed WE ARE A. "Now class, say it all together, 'We are a democracy.'"

We said it. Then Miss Gates said, "That's the difference between America and Germany. We are a democracy and Germany is a dictator-ship. Dictator-ship," she said. "Over here we don't believe in persecuting anybody. Persecution comes from people who are prejudiced. Pre-ju-dice," she enunciated carefully. "There are no better people in the world than the Jews, and why Hitler doesn't think so is a mystery to me." (Lee 280–81)

There are many questions we can ask after reading just this small passage. Think about where Scout's slogan, "Equal rights for all, special privileges for none," comes from. The fact that it is from a campaign slogan seems to add an air of superficiality to it, as if it is simply a piece of propaganda, rather than a tenet that people live by and hold themselves morally and ethically accountable to. Maybe this even equates democracy with Hitler's Germany in some ways, in the sense that propaganda seems to be a useful tool in both governments.

Consider other questions that could lead to an essay with a specific and intriguing argument: What has happened in the novel up to this point that gives this passage a very specific context? Would a classroom conversation about Hitler and democracy look and sound different today? How so? Why? Which elements of this dialogue are ironic? Why? What does Lee seem to want readers to understand or think about after reading this? How can you tell? How does this passage influence our characterization and opinion of Miss Gates? Why?

STRATEGIES

This section of the chapter addresses various possible topics for writing about the history and context of *To Kill a Mockingbird* as well as general methods for approaching these topics. These lists are in no way exhaustive and are meant to provide a jumping off point rather than an answer key. All topics discussed in this chapter could turn into successful essays, but use these suggestions to find your own ideas and form your own analyses.

History and Context

Studying history and context, as it relates to a novel, involves research, and you can begin by choosing a character, scene, theme, or setting and inquiring as to whether its presentation, portrayal, or description is reflective of this background and setting. Be aware that sometimes the time period in which the action of the book occurs can be different from the time in which the book was written and published, and even the difference of a few years can be significant. Once you have determined the similarities and differences between the real world and the world portrayed in the novel, you can begin to speculate about what Lee is trying to convey through her portrayal.

History and context might also pertain to the author's biography. Are there other details about Lee's life or beliefs that add depth and understanding to our reading of the novel? Was there anything in particular about Lee's life that led her to write *To Kill a Mockingbird*? If so, what bearing does Lee's life have on the novel? Did Lee have personal reasons for writing about race issues or the law? If so, how do those reasons surface, and what influence do they have on the book and/or its readers? If not, does this mean that Lee was purely a do-gooder, out to correct the evils of the world through her writing? Or was she simply capitalizing on topics she knew would interest readers and make her a wealthy woman and popular writer?

Is Lee able to blend reality and fiction in a way that makes them indistinguishable from each other? Another way to investigate the history and context of *To Kill a Mockingbird* is to research and evaluate how Lee's messages were received. Did any changes occur (whether direct or indirect) as a result of the novel? It can be enlightening to investigate who the original audience was for the work, what might have inspired Lee to write it, what readers' reactions were to the story, and how many incarnations the story has had.

Writing about the history and context of a novel is supported and supplemented by secondary sources and research. It is important to allow your essay topic to remain flexible, as the information you find through research might require you to alter, expand, or redirect your topic and intended argument. It is also important that you remain selective when writing. Do not include all of the history you find about the early twentieth century and/or Harper Lee. Choose only the most relevant details from your research to include in your essay and support them with your ideas and evidence from Lee's novel.

Sample Topics:

1. **Maycomb:** Is Maycomb a believable town? If not, does Lee purposely make it overly fictional? Why or why not?

   We know that Lee's hometown of Monroeville, Alabama, becomes Maycomb in the novel. Lee describes the town right at the beginning of the novel:

   > Maycomb was an old town, but it was a tired old town when I first knew it. In rainy weather the streets turned to red slop; grass grew on the sidewalks, the courthouse sagged in the square. . . . People moved slowly then. They ambled across the square, shuffled in and out of the stores around it, took their time about everything. A day was twenty-four hours long but seemed longer. There was no hurry, for there was nowhere to go, nothing to buy and no money to buy it with, nothing to see outside the boundaries of Maycomb County. But it was a time of vague optimism for some of the people: Maycomb County had recently been told that it had nothing to fear but fear itself. (Lee 5–6)

   How does this description help to pull readers in to the setting? Does Lee intentionally make the town almost like another character? How so? Why is it important to see Maycomb as a town and not a character, or vice versa? What details does this passage reveal about the town, the people, their politics?

2. **The South:** What changes would have to occur in the book in order for the setting to move out of the South?

   Compare Lee's novelization of the South with the actual events and standards of living at the time the novel is set. Does Lee take liberties, or is she portraying an accurate view of the American South at this time? In what ways do you see the setting specifically affecting or influencing the characters and their actions? What happens in the novel that would not

happen in other parts of the country or the world? Why? Why
is the novel regarded as universally appealing when the setting
is so specific? Are there elements of the American South that
people around the world in various time periods can relate to?
Is this true of other geographical areas, or is there something
particularly special about the South?

3. **Ku Klux Klan (KKK):** In what ways does the KKK provide a
   cultural background for the novel?

   Does it seem that Lee and/or her characters regard the KKK
   in a way that is too casual? Do they understand the threat the
   organization posed? There is discussion in the novel about the
   KKK being a reality of the past: "'Way back about nineteen-
   twenty there was a Klan, but it was a political organization
   more than anything. Besides, they couldn't find anybody to
   scare. They paraded by Mr. Sam Levy's house one night, but
   Sam just stood on his porch and told 'em things had come to a
   pretty pass, he'd sold 'em the very sheets on their backs. Sam
   made 'em so ashamed of themselves they went away. . . . The
   Ku Klux's gone. . . . It'll never come back'" (Lee 167). If racial
   issues are such a large part of the novel, why does Lee include
   this passage stating that the KKK has all but vanished? Does
   this contradict her other points about race, or does it somehow reinforce the book's negative attitude toward racism?

4. **Gender issues:** Are there points in the novel when gender
   becomes especially significant?

   What seems to be Lee's message about gender? Is it particularly significant that Scout is the girl, for example? How would
   the book be different if Jem were the main character/narra-
   tor? Why? What if the children were being raised by their
   mother, rather than their father, Atticus Finch? We know that
   in November 1962, "Nelle received her first honorary doctor-
   ate of letters" because she had "won the kind of recognition in

[her own field] that is customarily accorded to men" (Shields *Mockingbird* 220). Certainly Harper Lee's world would have been different without some of the gender inequity that she and others experienced. Do these issues find their way into the novel?

5. **The novel in its time(s):** Is it more important to study the time in which the novel is set or the time in which it was written and published?

Lee's presentation of historical facts in *To Kill a Mockingbird* bears some flaws:

> under scrutiny the novel's 1930s history is exposed as at times quite flawed in its presentation of facts. The WPA, for example, did not exist until 1935, but it is mentioned in the novel's fourth chapter, which is set in 1933. Eleanor Roosevelt did not violate segregation law by sitting with black audience members at the Southern Conference on Human Welfare in Birmingham until 1938, but this event is mentioned by Mrs. Merriweather during the fall of 1935. More important than these several occasional chronological lapses, however, is the novel's participation in racial and social ideology that characterized not the Depression era but the early civil rights era. Because the text's 1930s history is superficial, the novel is best understood as an amalgam or cross-historical montage, its 'historical present' diluted by the influence of events and ideology concurrent with its period of production. (Chura 1)

Do such errors affect our reading or opinions of the novel? Why or why not? In what ways can we situate the novel in its setting and/or time of publication in order to make more sense of the history as well as the novel itself?

6. **Scottsboro Boys:** To what extent are events in the book based on this real life group?

The Scottsboro Boys trials took place from 1931 to 1937 (Shields *Mockingbird* 117). Look for a reference resource such as Claudia Durst Johnson's *Understanding* To Kill a Mockingbird: *A Student Casebook to Issues, Sources, and Historic Documents* for more information about the Scottsboro Boys. Many assume that this is the case Lee is imitating in the novel, however, "Lee said that she did not have so sensational a case as the Scottsboro Boys in mind, 'but it will more than do as an example (albeit a lurid one) of deep-South attitudes on race vs. justice that prevailed at the time'" (Shields *Mockingbird* 118). Is Lee avoiding a fuller sense of life in the South at the time in her avoidance of depicting what became a sensationalistic case yet still emblematic of racial injustice in the South?

7. **Civil rights movement:** If a person read this novel without any knowledge of its author or publication history, would she or he be able to tell that it was written during the civil rights movement in the United States? Why or why not?

Think about the context of the novel's action as well as the context of the novel's initial publication—that is, the early years of the burgeoning civil rights movement. How did such historical realities affect the work's reception? Lee's biographer Charles J. Shields writes that "the novel, and the issues it treated, was a harbinger of change that had been on the horizon for years. Perhaps that's why it wasn't vilified more often: because it was part of a crescendo of ever-more-important events" (*Mockingbird* 197). Harper Lee said in an interview: "I don't think this business of getting on buses and flaunting state laws does much of anything. Except getting a lot of publicity, and violence. I think Reverend King and the NAACP are going about it in exactly the right way. The people in the South may not like it, but they respect it" (qtd. in Shields *Mockingbird* 223). It is both sad and fascinating to note that Atticus's role in preventing the lynching of Tom Robinson outside the jail is apparently unprecedented: "In two years of investigation, the exhibit researchers found no evidence of intervention by a white person to stop even a single lynching" (Saney 102). What role does this scene play in the novel as well as the world into which the novel was released? Why would Lee make up such a scene? How does the scene help us to better understand the characters, action, and historical context of the book?

8. **Emmett Till:** To what extent did Emmett Till's trial influence Lee's writing?

Emmett Till was "a 14-year-old boy from Chicago . . . [who] was brutally murdered by two white men in the Mississippi Delta on August 28, 1955 for allegedly whistling at a white woman in a store in Money, Mississippi" (Chura 2). Read Patrick Chura's article "Prolepsis and Anachronism: Emmett Till and the Historicity of *To Kill a Mockingbird*" in order to get a full idea of the links between Emmett Till and Tom Robinson. For example, "Emmett Till was killed on August 18, 1955 and . . . his body was found on August 31, dates which turn out to be practically identical to the date of Tom Robinson's death, which took place when 'August was on the brink of September'" (Chura 3). In a 1963 interview, Lee says, "in the book I tried to give a sense of proportion to life in the South, that there isn't a lynching before every breakfast. I think that Southerners react with the same kind of horror as other people do about the injustice in their land. In Mississippi, people were so revolted by what happened, they were so stunned, I don't think it will happen again" ("1963 Chicago"). Is she referring to the Emmett Till case/murder? Does it matter? How does knowing about the real situations influence our reading of the novel? Does Lee want readers to suspend their disbelief entirely and stay within the fictional confines of the novel, or does she want readers to note the similarities between Maycomb and the readers' own worlds? Why or why not?

Bibliography for History and Context

Chura, Patrick. "Prolepsis and Anachronism: Emmett Till and the Historicity of *To Kill a Mockingbird*." *Southern Literary Journal*, vol. 32, issue 2 (Spring 2000): 1–26.

Johnson, Claudia Durst. *Understanding* To Kill a Mockingbird: *A Student Casebook to Issues, Sources, and Historic Documents*. Westport, Conn.: Greenwood Press, 1994.

Lee, Harper. *To Kill a Mockingbird*. 1960. New York: Harper Perennial Modern Classics, 2006. Print.

Saney, Isaac. "Commentary: The Case Against *To Kill a Mockingbird*." *Race and Class*, vol. 45 (1): 99–110.

Shields, Charles J. *I Am Scout: The Biography of Harper Lee*. New York: Henry Holt and Company, 2008.

———. *Mockingbird: A Portrait of Harper Lee*. New York: Holt Paperbacks, 2007.

PHILOSOPHY AND IDEAS

READING TO WRITE

It is rare to find a novel that emphasizes or promotes only one philosophy or idea. Therefore, the search for philosophies and ideas within a book can be widely varied and deeply rewarding when you can make connections between the novel and the world it inhabits, in terms of the larger, perhaps even universal, ideas contained within it.

Consider the following passage when thinking about philosophy and ideas expressed or suggested in *To Kill a Mockingbird*. Certainly this is not the only place in the novel that deals with philosophical notions and ideas, but it provides a representative example:

> "But lots of folks have been hung—hanged—on circumstantial evidence," said Jem.
>
> "I know, and lots of 'em probably deserved it, too—but in the absence of eyewitnesses there's always a doubt, sometimes only the shadow of a doubt. The law says, 'reasonable doubt,' but I think a defendant's entitled to the shadow of a doubt. There's always the possibility, no matter how improbable, that he's innocent."
>
> "Then it all goes back to the jury, then. We oughta do away with juries." Jem was adamant.
>
> Atticus tried hard not to smile but couldn't help it. "You're rather hard on us, son. I think maybe there might be a better way. Change the law. Change it so that only judges have the power of fixing the penalty in capital cases."

"Then go up to Montgomery and change the law."

"You'd be surprised how hard that'd be. I won't live to see the law changed, and if you live to see it you'll be an old man."

This was not good enough for Jem. "No sir, they oughta do away with juries. He wasn't guilty in the first place and they said he was."

"If you had been on that jury, son, and eleven other boys like you, Tom would be a free man," said Atticus. "So far nothing in your life has interfered with your reasoning process. Those are twelve reasonable men in everyday life, Tom's jury, but you saw something come between them and reason. You saw the same thing that night in front of the jail. When that crew went away, they didn't go as reasonable men, they went because we were there. There's something in our world that makes men lose their heads—they couldn't be fair if they tried. In our courts, when it's a white man's word against a black man's, the white man always wins. They're ugly, but those are the facts of life."

"Doesn't make it right," said Jem stolidly. He beat his fist softly on his knee. "You can't just convict a man on evidence like that—you can't."

"You couldn't, but they could and did. The older you grow the more of it you'll see. The one place where a man ought to get a square deal is in a courtroom, be he any color of the rainbow, but people have a way of carrying their resentments right into a jury box. As you grow older, you'll see white men cheat black men every day of your life, but let me tell you something and don't you forget it—whenever a white man does that to a black man, no matter who he is, how rich he is, or how fine a family he comes from, that white man is trash."

Atticus was speaking so quietly his last word crashed on our ears. I looked up, and his face was vehement. "There's nothing more sickening to me than a low-grade white man who'll take advantage of a Negro's ignorance. Don't fool yourselves—it's all adding up and one of these days we're going to pay the bill for it. I hope it's not in you children's time." (Lee 250–52)

What sorts of philosophies does this excerpt express or suggest? How does it help us to learn more about Atticus and Jem? How does it help us to learn more about the philosophies and ideas of their world? Why is Atticus not more hopeful for the future? What do you imagine will become of Jem's views on life after such a conversation? Why does Atticus find it more reasonable to change the law than to change people's views and actions in regard to race? Why is it significant that Atticus is speaking quietly at the end of this passage? What does such a detail reveal about his beliefs, parenting style, and advocacy?

STRATEGIES

This section of the chapter addresses various possible topics for writing about philosophy and ideas in *To Kill a Mockingbird* as well as general methods for approaching these topics. These lists are in no way exhaustive and are meant to provide a jumping off point rather than an answer key. Use these suggestions to find your own ideas and form your own analyses.

Philosophy and Ideas

Analyzing a book's philosophical frame reveals how literature influences life and inspires a deeper level of thinking about more abstract topics concerning people's beliefs, behaviors, attitudes, and aspirations. Scholars look at Harper Lee to tell us about life in the South in the early twentieth century—not just in terms of what people did but how and what they thought and the insights those thoughts can offer.

This line of thinking allows you to look at *To Kill a Mockingbird* in a broad context. For example, is there such a thing as a philosophy of racism, and how does the story examine that? Some believe that the work is itself racist or enacts racist attitudes because it sets up black people as onlookers and stereotypes, rather than fully formed characters actively participating in the story and their lives. Is racism larger than the people who practice it and/or inhabit its world? Does it transcend humanity in a way that makes it inevitable? Part of human nature? Something people cannot control? What does Lee's book say about these ideas?

Writing about the philosophy and ideas in a book means that you identify broad philosophical notions and investigate the ways in which the book comments on them. Studying these concepts might necessitate research into topics such as the history of the philosophy and/or history of the time in which the work is set; you will then see more clearly how these ideas are linked with history and context as well as other areas of possible investigation and analysis. Supplemental research can be important, but a close reading of Lee's novel should be your focus. Do not make claims that cannot be supported by the words of the novel itself.

Sample Topics:

1. **Racism:** Are there degrees of racism?

   Does the book portray characters in a racist way? Does Lee seem to acknowledge that some racism, or some types of racism, are acceptable or inevitable? How can we explain the apparent contradiction between Atticus fighting for Tom Robinson's rights yet employing a black housekeeper?

2. **Importance of education:** What sort of philosophy of education does *To Kill a Mockingbird* promote?

   Atticus's most important lesson is repeated throughout the novel: "You never really understand a person until you consider things from his point of view . . . until you climb into his skin and walk around in it" (Lee 33). Does he teach this lesson by example? Which characters are willing and able to do this? Which are not? What message does Lee send by differentiating characters in this particular way?

3. **Gender roles:** What kind of power does Scout associate with Jem and Atticus, and what power does she associate with women? Does this change as the novel progresses?

   Consider the following comment about gender and race in the United States in the early twentieth century: "In this place and time, the word of a white woman counts more than that of a Black man" (Ware 288). Is the comment more revealing about race or about gender? In what ways is this philosophy evident in *To Kill a Mockingbird*? What does Lee seem to want to say about gender? Why? How can you tell? What does it mean to be a lady in the context of the novel? Does everyone have the same definition? To what extent are gender roles in the book a reflection of southern culture, and to what extent are the roles more universal?

4. **Written law versus moral law:** Are there laws that should be broken?

   Atticus explains to Scout why Ewells only go to school on the first day by saying, "Sometimes it's better to bend the law a little in special cases" (Lee 33). Does Atticus always acknowledge when laws need to be bent a little? Would he ever bend a law a lot or break one? Should he? Why or why not? Who holds the power in terms of written and moral laws? How are these people or institutions regarded by the characters and by Lee?

5. **Respect:** Who is supposed to be showing respect to whom, and how does Lee indicate when the respect shown is unearned or undeserved?

   Atticus tells Scout that the people who think he is wrong to defend Tom Robinson are "'entitled to full respect for their opinions.'" But are they, really? Does Lee think so? How can you tell? Are there characters that she wants us to disrespect? Why? How does she convey this?

6. **Wisdom:** Are any of the characters in *To Kill a Mockingbird* truly wise? How do you define the term?

   Certainly the novel emphasizes education, in the standard classroom form as well as insight gleaned by learning from life experience. Do either of these types of education lead to wisdom in the novel? How so, or why not? How is wisdom in the novel different from knowledge? In what ways do characters make use of their knowledge or wisdom?

7. **Religion:** What is the role of religion in *To Kill a Mockingbird*?

The children attend church with Calpurnia, and it is an eye-opening experience for them. Is this the novel's only foray into religion, or does it surface in other ways? Does the courtroom ever resemble a church? Atticus is modeled in part after Lee's father, A.C., who once confronted a pastor who chose to include a pro–civil rights message in his sermon: "It may . . . surprise admirers of Atticus Finch that the man he was modeled after did not believe that a church pulpit was the proper place for preaching about racial equity" (Shields *Mockingbird* 121). Does the novel demonstrate a general tension between religion and civil rights?

8. **Real versus ideal:** How do individual characters tell the difference between the real and the ideal? What do their methods and their opinions reveal about them?

There are discrepancies between what people say they believe and what they actually live by. Do these discrepancies indicate a simple lack of empathy or something else entirely? Harper Lee said that "People generally see what they look for, and hear what they listen for" (Lee 198). Is this true for the characters? How so?

9. **Empathy:** Which characters in the novel show the most empathy? How are we supposed to feel about these characters, and how are our feelings affected by their capacity to empathize? One of the repeated lessons in the novel is this: "Atticus was right. One time he said you never really know a man until you stand in his shoes and walk around in them. Just standing on the Radley porch was enough" (Lee 321). Earlier in the novel, Atticus says, "'you children last night made Walter Cunningham stand in my shoes for a minute. That was enough'" (Lee 179). There are several instances in the novel that deal with ideas of empathy and compassion. Which characters promote this way of thinking? How does Lee want readers to feel about those characters, and how can we tell? What happens to characters who do not exercise compassion or empathy?

Bibliography for Philosophy and Ideas

Lee, Harper. *To Kill a Mockingbird*. 1960. New York: Harper Perennial Modern Classics, 2006. Print.

Shields, Charles J. *I Am Scout: The Biography of Harper Lee*. New York: Henry Holt and Company, 2008.

——. *Mockingbird: A Portrait of Harper Lee*. New York: Holt Paperbacks, 2007.

Ware, Michele S. "'Just a Lady': Gender and Power in Harper Lee's *To Kill a Mockingbird*." In *Women in Literature: Reading Through the Lens of Gender*. Eds. Jerilyn Fisher and Ellen S. Silber. Westport, Conn.: Greenwood Press, 2003. 286–88.

COMPARISON
AND CONTRAST

READING TO WRITE

A careful reader can make many comparisons or find contrasts between various elements in the novel as well as between the novel and other forms of the novel, such as film adaptations, or other books or cultural expressions. Think about possible comparisons and contrasts you can find within or suggested by the following passage:

> People moved slowly then. They ambled across the square, shuffled in and out of the stores around it, took their time about everything. A day was twenty-four hours long but seemed longer. There was no hurry, for there was nowhere to go, nothing to buy and no money to buy it with, nothing to see outside the boundaries of Maycomb County. But it was a time of vague optimism for some of the people: Maycomb County had recently been told that it had nothing to fear but fear itself.
>
> We lived on the main residential street in town—Atticus, Jem and I, plus Calpurnia our cook. Jem and I found our father satisfactory: he played with us, read to us, and treated us with courteous detachment.
>
> Calpurnia was something else again. She was all angles and bones; she was nearsighted; she squinted; her hand was as wide as a bed slat and twice as hard. She was always ordering me out of the kitchen, asking me why I couldn't behave as well as Jem when she knew he was older, and calling me home when I wasn't ready to come. Our battles were epic and one-sided. Calpurnia always won, mainly because Atticus always took

her side. She had been with us ever since Jem was born, and I had felt her tyrannical presence as long as I could remember.

Our mother died when I was two, so I never felt her absence. She was a Graham from Montgomery; Atticus met her when he was first elected to the state legislature. He was middle-aged then, she was fifteen years his junior. Jem was the product of their first year of marriage; four years later I was born, and two years later our mother died from a sudden heart attack. They said it ran in her family. I did not miss her, but I think Jem did. He remembered her clearly, and sometimes in the middle of a game he would sigh at length, then go off and play by himself behind the car-house. When he was like that, I knew better than to bother him. (Lee 6–7)

When exactly is the *then* referred to at the beginning of the passage? How does this time period differ from the one in which the book was written and published? How would the original readers of *To Kill a Mockingbird* see themselves in comparison to the people of Maycomb County during the time in which the novel is set? Why? How does the setting of the novel compare to today? How can readers still find ways to relate to a time and way of living that seem so different from their own?

How do Maycomb County and the time period in which the novel is set compare to what is happening in the rest of the country at that time? What would be different if the novel was set in the present day? What other famous presidential quotes from the twentieth and twenty-first centuries could be applied to the novel, and how would they compare with the ways in which "nothing to fear but fear itself" reflects the action and messages of the novel?

Do Atticus, Jem, Scout, and Calpurnia make up a typical family structure for their time and place? Why or why not? Why does Lee choose this particular family makeup for the Finches? Would the Finches be more typical in or representative of today's world—or less? Why? What do readers today think of this description of Atticus's parenting style? What would Lee's first readers have thought of it, and why? How do changing attitudes about Atticus's parenting reflect changing attitudes about parenting in general?

In what ways does the third paragraph of this excerpt ask readers to compare Scout's childhood experiences with their own? Why would Lee want readers to do this? What might the results of such comparisons be, and why?

How can this passage help us to find ways to compare and contrast Jem and Scout? Is this background information necessary for such comparisons?

Writing papers that compare or contrast forms or elements of a novel can allow us to dig deeply into the components that we are comparing or contrasting. It is imperative that the paper contain a well-developed conclusive statement, rather than simply listing similarities and differences for their own sake.

STRATEGIES

This section of the chapter addresses various possible topics for writing about comparisons and contrasts within *To Kill a Mockingbird* as well as general methods for approaching these topics. Use these suggestions to find your own ideas and form your own analyses. These lists are in no way exhaustive and are meant to provide a jumping off point rather than an answer key.

Comparison and Contrast

Writing a paper that compares and/or contrasts elements of the novel involves much more than simply listing similarities and differences between or among two or more things. These lists might help you early in the drafting process, but your essay eventually needs to move beyond this point to discuss why these similarities and/or differences are notable and important to the novel. You would do well to ask questions such as, Does Lee intentionally set up some comparisons in order to perhaps show different points of view or circumstances? Do we notice particular comparisons and contrasts simply because of the time in which we live and our perceptions of life in the early twentieth century?

One of the most interesting things you can do with this approach to an essay is to make a comparison between two or more elements/characters that on the surface seem very similar. The more surprising your comparison or contrast is, the more engaging your paper could be to your readers (provided you back up your argument with sufficient evidence from the text). You cannot make a comparison or contrast statement based solely on your own perceptions and "feelings" about the work. Whatever claim you decide to make must be supported by the text itself.

Sample Topics:

1. **Harper Lee and Truman Capote:** Are there indications in their writing itself that Lee and Capote were close friends?

   Compare *To Kill a Mockingbird* with *In Cold Blood*. Is the writing similar? The style? Content? Is Lee's helpfulness with *In Cold Blood* evident? Is Capote's influence on *To Kill a Mockingbird* obvious? Read Charles Shields's biographies on Harper Lee as well as biographies of and works by Truman Capote in order to make nuanced comparisons.

2. **Harper Lee and Jane Austen:** Can Lee's writing be traced directly to Austen's?

   Lee once said that "all [she wanted] to be is the Jane Austen of south Alabama" (Newquist 412). Is she? Austen is a nineteenth-century writer known for her character-driven novels about her small section of English society. Is this similar to what Lee does? Why do you think Lee would set this goal for herself? What sort of example did Austen set that Lee would want to follow? Are the two women writers really more different than they are alike? Would Austen have approved of Lee's novel?

3. **Childhood and adulthood:** What sorts of transitions (if any) does Lee provide between representations of childhood and adulthood in the novel?

   After the night at the jail, Scout remembers, "The full meaning of the night's events hit me and I began crying" (Lee 177). Could the full meaning of the events really have hit her then, or might they have sunk in only later?

4. **Harper Lee and Scout Finch:** Is it immediately obvious that Scout is modeled on Lee herself, or is she strictly a fictional character?

Do some research on Harper Lee, perhaps beginning with Charles Shields's books *Mockingbird* or *I Am Scout*, to help you determine any similarities between Lee and Scout. The title of Shields's book seems to indicate that Scout undoubtedly shares characteristics with Lee. Is this evident in the novel itself? If so, where? If not, how do we find their shared characteristics, if there are any?

5. **The real Boo Radley and the one the children and town residents have invented:** Do we ever really learn the truth about Boo Radley? Is it important?

During their childhood,

> Jem gave a reasonable description of Boo: Boo was about six-and-a-half feet tall, judging from his tracks; he dined on raw squirrels and any cats he could catch, that's why his hands were blood-stained—if you ate an animal raw, you could never wash the blood off. There was a long jagged scar that ran across his face; what teeth he had were yellow and rotten; his eyes popped, and he drooled most of the time. (Lee 14)

What does the word *reasonable* tell us about the children and the way that they see their world? Are there people or ideas in Maycomb that support or counter the ways in which the children see Boo at the beginning of the novel? At the end? How does Lee want readers to feel about Boo Radley when we first meet him and throughout the novel? Does she want our perceptions of Boo to change? How can you tell? What do other characters' relationships to Boo reveal about those characters? Is Boo ever a true character in his own right, or is he only there to help reflect others' true natures?

6. **A.C. Lee and Atticus Finch:** To what extent is it important to know that Lee modeled Atticus on her own father?

Charles Shields, Lee's biographer, writes that "A.C. was a fond and indulgent father" (*Mockingbird* 58). Can Atticus be described in the same way? Why or why not? How central to the novel is Atticus's role as a father? In what ways would the book and its themes have to change if Atticus was simply a member of the same community, rather than the single father of Jem and Scout? We know that "Mr. Lee's attitudes toward child raising were similar to that of the hero of Nelle's novel, Atticus Finch. He spoke to his children in an adultlike manner, extending them the privilege to think and reply like grown-ups. They loved him for this mark of respect" (Shields *I Am* 18). Does Lee ever seem critical of Atticus and the way that he raises his children, reflecting perhaps some dissatisfaction with her own childhood? Does Lee's portrayal of Atticus lead us to believe that she worships her father as a hero or a saint? In what ways might that help us to better understand the novel?

7. **Film and novel:** Is the film a reasonable adaptation of the novel? Why or why not?

Which characters are at the center of the novel? Which characters are at the center of the film? If there are differences between the two, how do those differences change the major concerns of the film and novel (such as themes, philosophies, ideas, and points of view)? Is the film and/or novel atypical from others of its era? How so? What does this reveal about the writers, actors, characters, or general content and themes? Are there characters that you like better in the film or the novel? Why? How does this change the book's/film's tone or its message? At first, the book was a series of vignettes rather than one seamless story. To what extent is the film also a series of vignettes? Do the film and novel invest in social criticism in the same ways? Do they attack the same issues in the same ways? Why or why not? For further information, look at *To Kill a Mockingbird: The Screenplay and Related Readings.*

Bibliography for Comparison and Contrast

Lee, Harper. *To Kill a Mockingbird.* 1960. New York: Harper Perennial Modern Classics, 2006. Print.

Shields, Charles J. *I Am Scout: The Biography of Harper Lee.* New York: Henry Holt and Company, 2008.

———. *Mockingbird: A Portrait of Harper Lee.* New York: Holt Paperbacks, 2007.

To Kill a Mockingbird: The Screenplay and Related Readings. Evanston, Ill.: McDougall Littell, 1997.

INDEX

Characters in *To Kill a Mockingbird* are indexed by first name.